THE COMPLETE BOOK OF CHALK LETTERING

CREATE AND DEVELOP YOUR OWN STYLE

VALERIE McKEEHAN

Workman Publishing

New York

COPYRIGHT © 2015 BY LILY & VAL, LLC

All rights reserved. No portion of this book may be reproduced—mechanically, electronically, or by any other means, including photocopying—without written permission of the publisher. Published simultaneously in Canada by Thomas Allen & Son Limited.

Library of Congress Cataloging-in-Publication Data is available.

ISBN 978-0-7611-8611-3

Cover Design by Colleen AF Venable
Design by Tae Won Yu

Photography credits: Chasing Eden Photography (page 15), Heather Nan Photography (page 27)

Workman books are available at special discounts when purchased in bulk for premiums and sales promotions as well as for fund-raising or educational use. Special editions of book excerpts can also be created to specification. For details, contact the Special Sales Director at the address below or send an email to specialmarkets@workman.com.

WORKMAN PUBLISHING CO., INC.
225 VARICK STREET
NEW YORK, NY 10014-4381
WORKMAN.COM

WORKMAN is a registered trademark of Workman Publishing Co., Inc.

Printed in China

First printing September 2015

10 9 8 7 6 5 4 3 2 1

TO MY HUSBAND, MAK,
FOR ENCOURAGING AND SUPPORTING
ME FROM THE VERY BEGINNING OF THIS
CHALKY ADVENTURE.

Contents

APEX

CAP HEIC

CROSSBAR

An

serifs
(foot)

OF

BAR

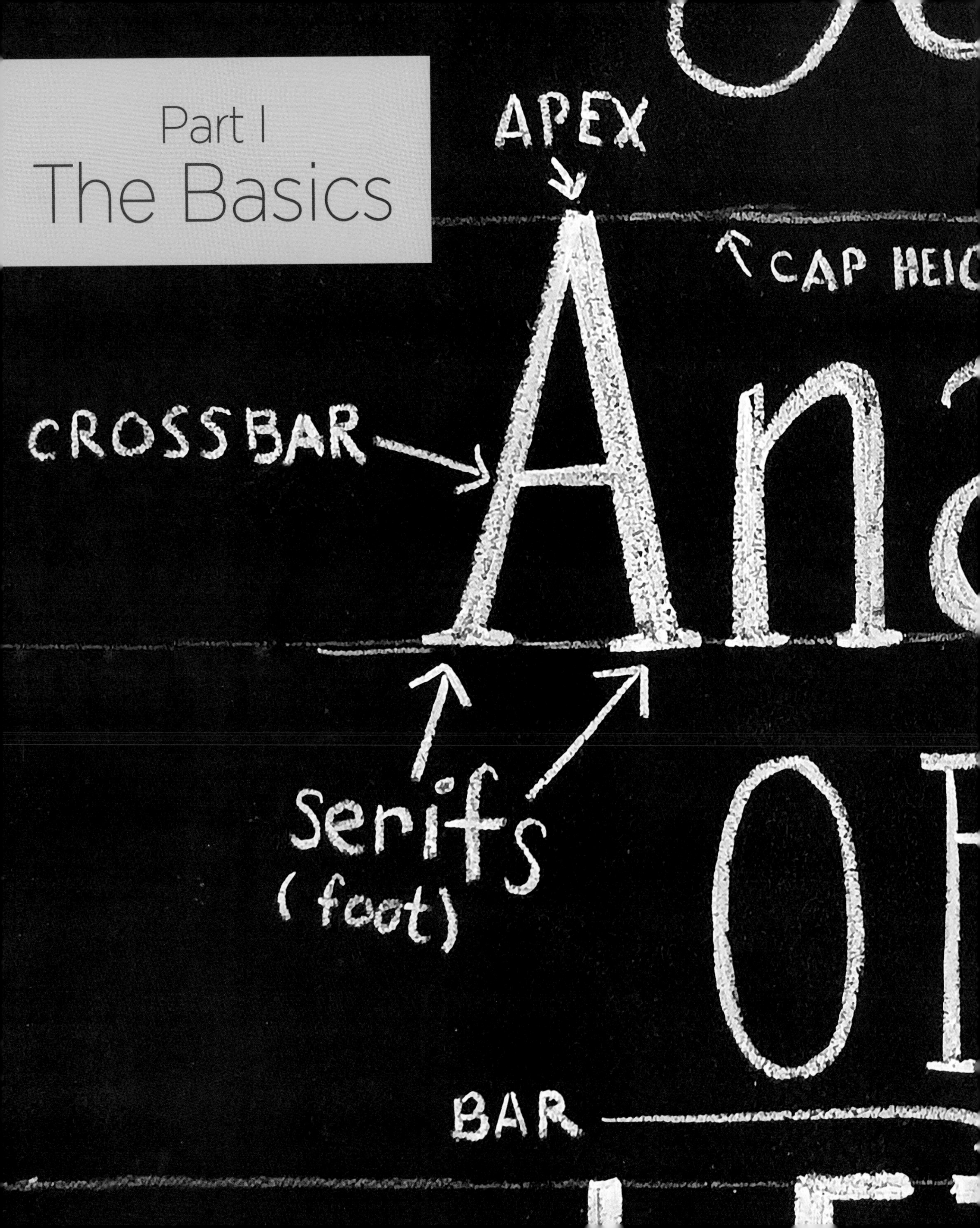

STROKE

BOWL

atomy

FINIALS

Chapter 1

The ABCs of Chalk Lettering

Creating your own chalk lettering starts with a basic knowledge of letterforms. This will be the first and the most important layer in your creations. However, before we can jump right in, you'll need to learn a few things first.

What You Need

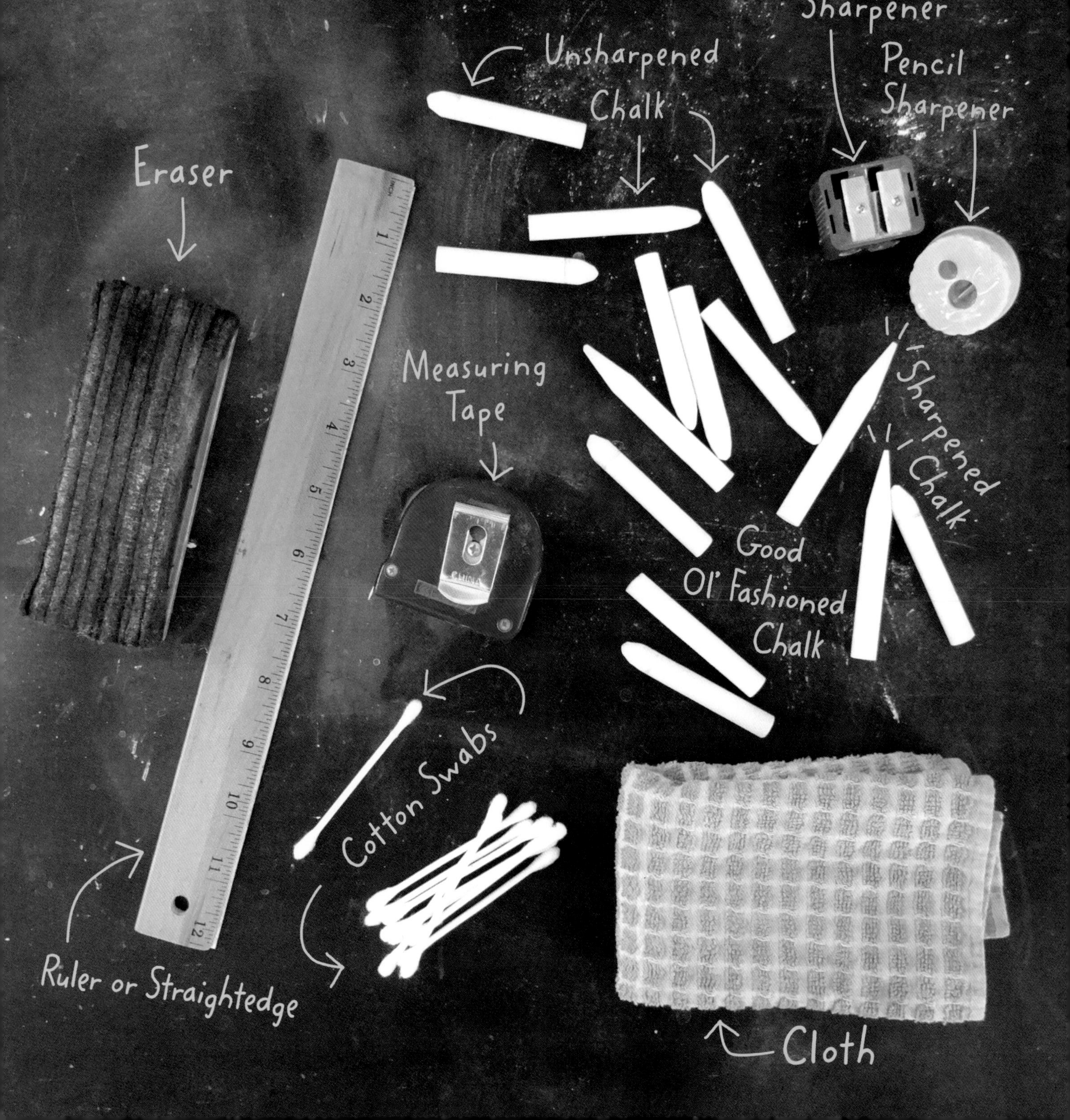

Eraser

Unsharpened Chalk

Eyeliner Sharpener

Pencil Sharpener

Measuring Tape

Sharpened Chalk

Good Ol' Fashioned Chalk

Cotton Swabs

Cloth

Ruler or Straightedge

Part of the charm of chalk art is that it doesn't require much in terms of tools. You will find a practice chalkboard panel on the front inside flap of this book with ready-to-go guidelines for practicing anytime, as well as two others in the back. The other necessary items are lightweight, easily transportable, and inexpensive. What's not to love?

Good Old-Fashioned Chalk

A standard piece of white chalk will work just fine. I wouldn't recommend using sidewalk chalk as the thickness will be difficult to maneuver on the panels of this book. My personal preference is Crayola Anti-Dust Chalk. Don't let the name fool you! It certainly creates dust, but I've found this chalk to be heavier and denser, which provides a lovely vibrancy when used on your chalkboard.

While we're on the topic of dust, let me just say, it is a great thing! Most of my days are spent covered in it. As you draw, dust specks will inevitably accumulate on your work. I am constantly lightly blowing on the board to remove these specks. Because of this, you may want to be conscious of where you are working.

A Pencil Sharpener or Eyeliner Sharpener

This tool is one of my biggest trade secrets! People are often shocked when they find out that you can sharpen chalk. It's something so simple, yet it will make all the difference for your drawings. Any pencil sharpener or eyeliner sharpener will work, as long as it has two holes. This is a critical element. The smaller hole will work for sharpening your pencil when you are sketching ideas in your sketchbook. The larger hole will fit your chalk perfectly (sizes are pretty much standard—about ½ inch wide).

A Felt Eraser and a Cloth Rag

A felt eraser will erase the lettering, but it will not completely take away the dust. Instead, it will disperse a dusty cloud around your board. In contrast, a cloth rag, which at different times can be used damp or dry, will remove any unwanted dust entirely. A specific type of rag is not necessary. A piece of an old T-shirt or a washcloth will do.

Cotton Swabs

Instead of erasing the entire design and starting again, sometimes all you need to do is correct a portion. A cotton swab will give you precise, ninja-like erasing abilities.

A Ruler or Straightedge

The front practice panel of this book conveniently already contains drawn guidelines. However, a ruler will come in handy, especially as you are learning the different layout techniques in Chapter 2. In addition to a 12-inch ruler, I like using a 6-inch plastic one that easily fits in my bag. Bonus: It can double-duty as a bookmark! At times, it may also be helpful to have a small tape measure handy.

Preparing Your Chalkboards

Before you begin drawing, it is necessary to "season" your chalkboard. Chalkboard seasoning sounds fancy, but it simply involves rubbing the side of a piece of chalk over the entire chalkboard and then erasing. A chalkboard that has been seasoned will appear a bit scratched, muted, and gray in color, as opposed to flat, stark, and black.

When you are seasoning a brand-new chalkboard, like the panels at the front and back of this book, you may need to wear off some of the protective coating on the chalk beforehand. Just rub the chalk on any hard surface.

It might take a bit of rubbing to get the chalk to transfer to your board at first, but once it does, keep going until it's completely covered. Wipe the board clean with your cloth rag.

The purpose of seasoning a chalkboard isn't just to create a rustic look, but to prepare the surface for handling chalk. An unseasoned chalkboard runs the risk of the chalk "burning" into the surface, leaving a permanent mark. The chalk on a seasoned chalkboard will remove cleanly over and over again.

Getting to the Point

Open one of the three chalkboard flaps on this book and draw a line with a blunt piece of unsharpened chalk. Now, sharpen another piece of chalk and draw a second line with the pointy edge. Notice the difference in the texture of the lines' edges. The blunt chalk will provide a rough, broken edge. The sharp chalk will deliver a tight, more exact line. As you continue to use the sharpened chalk, observe how it wears down to a dull point. Continue drawing lines, but vary your pressure. When you apply heavy pressure, the result is a bright white line as opposed to a lighter, more textured line when soft pressure is applied.

→ DULL POINT

→ BLUNT

→ SHARP

→ Heavy Pressure

Lowdown on Letters

Now let's get a bit technical with letters. It's helpful to know these terms when learning and appreciating hand-lettering since using phrases like "that small line-thing at the top of the thick vertical line" gets a bit confusing.

Crossbars and Cross Strokes

Welcome the letters "f" and "t" with open arms. They'll give you the ability to draw fun cross strokes varying from short and rigid to long and swirly. The crossbars on the capitals "A" and "H" are equally as versatile.

Ascenders and Descenders

A gorgeously flowing descender is enough to make me weak in the knees! Look for the lowercase letters "g," "y," "p," and "f" as opportunities for descender practice and the lowercase letters "f," "t," "h," "k," "l," and "b" for ascender practice.

Serifs

Serifs play a huge role in completely altering the feel of a word. Play with varying thicknesses and styles. Try a slab serif, or thick letters with a thin serif, or vice versa. Instead of a straight line, draw wave-shaped serifs.

Baselines

Varying baselines in your design is a great way to achieve new looks. Straight baselines will feel more traditional while wavy or otherwise uneven baselines contribute to a whimsical feel.

Entry and Exit Points

Begin your words with a pronounced entry point or take advantage of an exit point to add interest and style. The points where your letters connect with other letters are also key positions to vary.

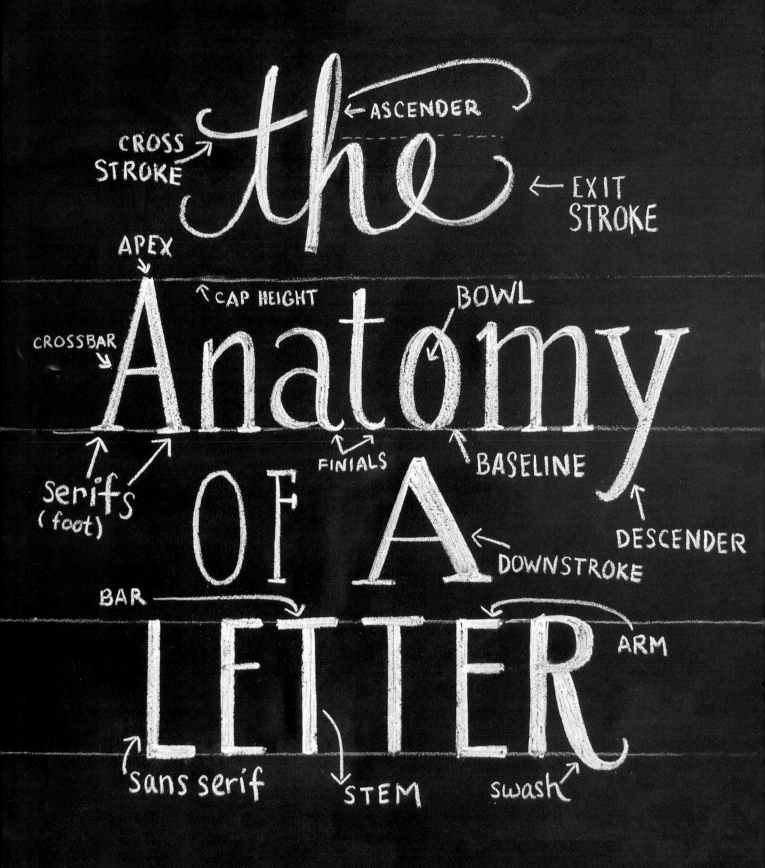

The Big Three:
Sans Serif, Serif, and Script Lettering Styles

To get started drawing letters, you'll need to familiarize yourself with the basic shapes and characteristics of three standard lettering styles: sans serif, serif, and script. Each style can be broken into multiple subcategories and classifications, but we will be sticking with the basics for now. After you become comfortable, you can begin taking liberties with your letters and creating your own unique styles.

Don't worry if your attempts at lettering aren't exact. We are all unique, original individuals, and our hand-lettering will reflect this. Our letters will be off. They will be imperfect and beautiful. That's the allure of it! Always remember: The beauty is in the imperfection.

The idea here is to familiarize yourself with the basic shape, concept, and overall style of these three lettering styles. Again, this is just your base. Becoming proficient in standard shapes of letterforms will help you develop your own unique style.

Sans Serif

CHARACTERISTICS

- Without serifs. *Sans* is a French word meaning "without."

- Little to zero width variation among strokes.

- Considered a more modern style.

- Often used for online text since reading letters without serifs is considered to be easier when displayed on-screen.

Serif

CHARACTERISTICS

- Includes serifs or small strokes at the ends of the vertical and horizontal strokes of the letters.

- Considered a more traditional style.

- Widely used for "body text" (the main portion of a printed piece, words excluding the headline or footnotes) and considered easier to read.

Script

CHARACTERISTICS

- Features joined lowercase letters.

- Designed to resemble handwriting.

- Can be formal or casual.

- My personal favorite typeface to manipulate.

Hello, My Name Is
How to Draw a Sans Serif Style

Channel your inner six-year-old and using sans serif style, roughly sketch the letters of your name on your practice panel. Be aware of the spacing between your letters, keeping it consistent.

1 Use the guides on your practice panel to familiarize yourself with drawing on a straight line (your baseline) and making each of your letters the same height (your cap height). Part of the fun of hand-lettering will be creating words with varied cap heights and baselines, but for now, try to be exact.

2 Once you have roughly chalked in where the letters will go, make multiple passes with your chalk to complete the outline of the shape. Chalk lettering involves making multiple changes to each letter as opposed to calligraphy where the thickness and style is contingent upon how much pressure you apply. As your chalk begins to dull, you may need to give it a few turns in the sharpener. A sharp edge will be more precise.

3 Now that the shape outlines are completed, a dull piece of chalk can be used to fill them in!

Know Your ABCs
How to Draw a Serif Style

This time, let's start with the beginning of the alphabet drawn in a serif typeface. Feel like you're back in elementary school?

1 Start out drawing the basic shape of the letters just like we did with the sans serif style.

2 Once you have the letters "ABCD" roughly drawn, go back over the letters to thicken those downstrokes. When drawing a serif type, be aware of the thick strokes versus thin strokes. Your downstrokes should be thicker. This adds to the classic, traditional feel of a serif font.

3 With a sharp piece of chalk, add the serif to the top and bottom of the strokes. For a different effect, connect the serif to the body of the stroke by drawing a small, curved, diagonal connector. This is called a bracketed serif and will give the letter a completely different look.

Perfectly Scripted
How to Draw a Script Style

Now, for my favorite type of lettering, the script typeface. Let's begin with the word "Sweet."

1 Roughly draw each letter connecting the "ee" and the "t." Take your time as you create this initial pass of letters. This will become the underlying structure of your word. Throughout any of these practice exercises, erase often and redraw! The ability to erase is one of the best parts about chalk lettering.

2 Once you are happy with the structure, go back over the letterforms to thicken the downstrokes. This adds a calligraphic style to your script lettering. To get this effect requires multiple passes on the letters. Keep the exit strokes and upstrokes thin, for an elegant contrast.

The Handwriting Myth

I want to dispose of a myth I hear quite regularly. It goes something like this: "I don't have good handwriting! I could never write letters like *that*." Or, "Your chalk art is so beautiful. You must have the best handwriting." Wrong and wrong! Naturally good handwriting is not an indicator of success with chalk lettering and design. If you're among those of us with poor handwriting (myself included—it's true!), there's no need to worry. Unlike traditional forms of calligraphy, which require precise swoops and continuous lettering flow, chalk art involves drawing. Instead of thinking about a letter as a letter, think of the letter as a shape. I've found that this simple mind-shift can have a profound impact.

A FEW HELPFUL TERMS

Typography refers to typeset letters; the arrangement, style, or appearance of printed letters on a page.

Calligraphy refers to writing; the art of producing decorative handwriting or handwritten lettering.

Lettering refers to drawing; the art of drawing letters. Our time spent in this book will be discussing the art of hand-lettering in chalk.

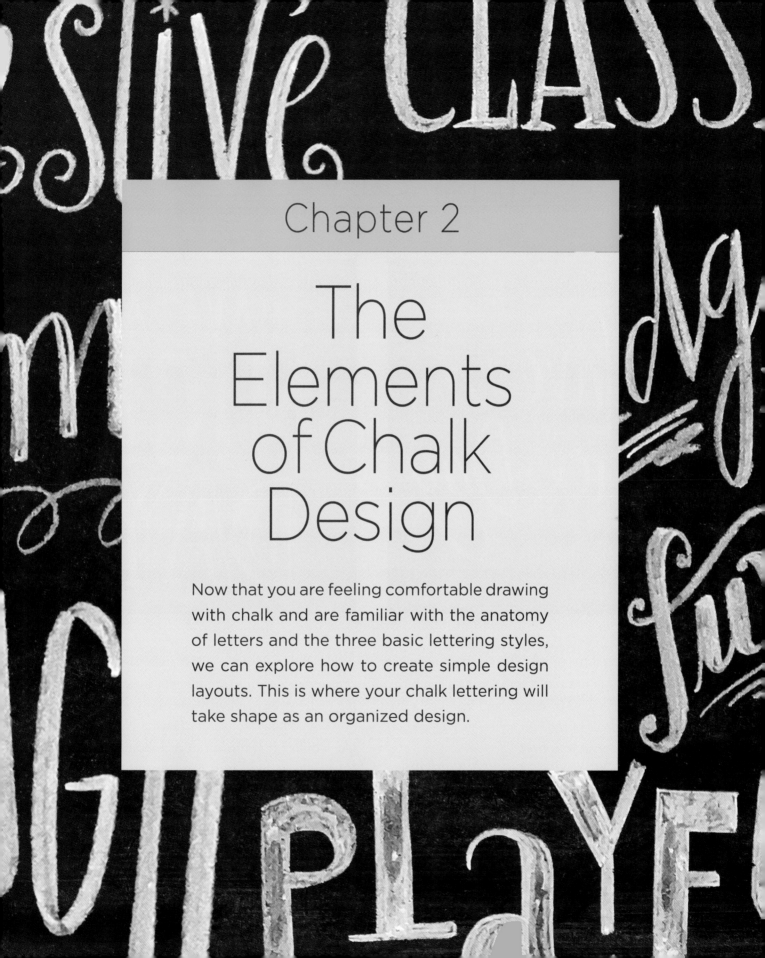

Chapter 2

The Elements of Chalk Design

Now that you are feeling comfortable drawing with chalk and are familiar with the anatomy of letters and the three basic lettering styles, we can explore how to create simple design layouts. This is where your chalk lettering will take shape as an organized design.

Choosing Lettering Styles

A

B

When creating a layout, you must first decide what lettering styles to use and, if you're using a combination of styles, how to combine them into a cohesive piece. Your choice of style (or styles) will depend on the mood you want to convey.

Often, the phrase you choose to draw will determine the attitude of the piece so start with one that inspires you and be aware of how it makes you feel. However, the words themselves are only a small part of the equation. The rest of the communication is delivered through style—your style! The same words can convey a completely different meaning depending on how you manipulate them.

Notice how the words "Have a Nice Day" feel like a different sentiment in each example. The first "Have a Nice Day" feels pleasant and light. On the other hand, the second "HAVE A NICE DAY" feels bold and strong. Despite the actual words, both convey distinctly different messages. You are in control of this message. Pretty powerful, right?

What Are Your Words *Really Saying?*

Here are several possible adjectives for describing the tone of your chalk lettering, just to name a few!

BOLD Festive Edgy

CONFIDENT Sophisticated

HIP ROUGH RETRO

Ornate VINTAGE

Finding Inspiration, Sketching Designs

How do you find inspiration? For me, it is a matter of keeping my eyes open. I try to visually soak in my surroundings wherever I am. Look for sources outside the realm of chalk art and lettering: the pattern on a vintage dress, the ornate railing on a building, a hot chocolate tin, antique books. Notice everything!

Of course, it is inevitable that you will be inspired by the work of others. The world is filled with hand-letterers, calligraphy artists, and typographers who do gorgeous art. It is easy to become enamored with a particular artist, but if you are constantly seeking out that person's designs as inspiration for your own, you'll never develop your own style. Instead, pick out elements you like in their work and use them as jumping-off points in your own. Maybe you love the way a certain artist uses a loopy descender. Take that bit of inspiration and draw a new piece based on that one detail.

But What Do I Want My Design to Say?

Half the battle in creating new chalk designs lies in finding a phrase or quote to draw. Most of the time the quote will dictate or greatly allude to a particular mood so deciding first on wording can be helpful.

Be aware of sentiments and phrases you use in your everyday life or search online for quotes to get you started. (Just be aware of copyright laws if you plan on selling any of your designs.) Of course, writing your own quotes is always desirable and will enrich the uniqueness of your pieces.

Pencil and Paper Sketches

Once you've found inspiration for a design, a phrase to draw, and which lettering styles you might want to use, work through the design with pencil and paper. My pencil sketches are never detailed or polished, but they allow me to know if a layout is going to "work" (see page 23) and determine which lettering styles I should use.

During your sketching stage you should establish two basic points:

1 What is the overall mood for the design?

2 How will the letters fit together to create a pleasing aesthetic?

Even when I am confident about an envisioned layout, I like to take thirty seconds to scribble it out on paper first.

Placing Chalk Guides

When creating a layout on a blank board, spending a few moments adding the following markings will keep your design lined up. It will also save you the irritation of drawing a design only to find there isn't enough space to complete it.

Before you begin, you must know the size of the chalkboard you are working with.

Here's how to place chalk guides:

1 Measure the center points on the top and bottom of the board and place a chalk mark. Likewise, measure the center points on the left and right sides and place a mark.

2 Find the center of the entire board by placing a mark where the vertical center and horizontal center lines you just drew meet.

3 Add a margin on all four corners. On each corner, measure ½ to 1 inch from the top and ½ to 1 inch from the side and place a bracket mark where the measurements collide. This will ensure you have an equal amount of space left around the drawing.

4 Add the guidelines that will determine where the elements in your design are placed. These lines are based on the pencil sketch and should be lightly drawn to ensure they will easily erase once the letters are drawn. For words that require a straight baseline, chalk in the line using your ruler. Estimate where each word will be placed and leave empty spaces to fill in the other words in your layout. The more you practice, the more you will get a feel for how much space to leave.

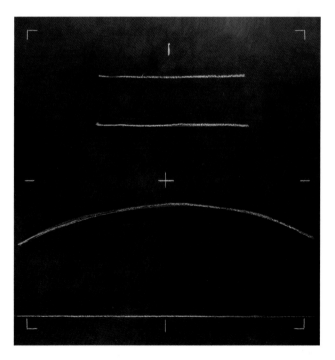

Principles of Design

As you know by now, I am a huge supporter of drawing chalk designs with minimal rules. At the same time, there are a few principles of good design that will prove extremely beneficial in your work. Here are the main things to keep in mind before getting started on your layout.

Emphasis

The human eye is drawn to focal points. This is why we have titles in magazine articles and headlines in advertisements. Emphasize key words in your design to add interest. Designs without emphasis or with the wrong emphasis are confusing and hard to read.

Spacing

If the letters, words, or lines between text are too squished together, your message will be hard to read—or look like a hash tag! If you leave too much space between them, your phrase will appear disconnected and confusing.

Blackboard Space

In graphic design, this is called "white space." But since we are working on a chalkboard, I've changed it to blackboard space. It refers to the negative space, the space where designed elements do not exist: the blank portions of your layout. The lack of design is, in fact, designed to help you achieve emphasis and, most important, balance. Disproportionate blackboard space can contribute to a lack of balance.

Repetition

Repetition makes all the different elements of the piece feel as if they belong together. For example, you may want to repeat the same lettering style on multiple words or repeat a similar flourish throughout a design. Designs that have zero repetitive elements will appear chaotic. For example, using too many different lettering styles causes a confusing end result.

Balance

I would argue this is the most important principle of good design. Do not confuse balance with symmetry. A symmetrical design is completely centered with the same elements on either side. A balanced drawing isn't necessarily symmetrical. Its elements can be varied and interesting, such as a banner, illustration, or flourish, but the overall piece will still look cohesive and put together. Balance involves the weight of your design being distributed evenly by the placement of each drawn element.

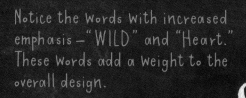

Design Dissected

Notice the Words With increased emphasis—"WILD" and "Heart." These Words add a Weight to the overall design.

If I took away the heart to the left of the Word "at," you'd notice a heaviness on the right side of the design.

The top and bottom Words have a similar lettering style.

The less pronounced Words "Stay" and "AT" are anchored by the flowers, vines, and hearts.

By using repetition, the vine theme is found in key areas through the piece making it appear cohesive and balanced.

Similarly, the flourish at the bottom adds a completed touch. Without it, the design Would feel awkward and uneven in comparison to the top half.

Friendspiration
How to Design a Chalk Layout

Let's practice drawing a chalk layout considering our newly learned principles of design.

Here are three rough pencil sketches of a few possible combinations of the words "Let's Be Friends Forever," keeping the principles of good design in mind.

Let's choose the first one. You can try your hand at the other two later.

It may be helpful to continue using the practice panel on the inside front cover. It will help you keep a straight baseline when necessary. However, if you feel comfortable, move to one of the practice panels without the printed guides. Just remember to draw in the chalk guidelines you learned on page 21. Use a straightedge for words that require a straight baseline.

1 After placing the guidelines, add key words. Key words will determine the spacing of the words around them. Adding these words is the hardest part of the design. If they are off, the whole design will be off. In this example, the key word is "Friends." Lightly add the word "Friends" in a script style. Notice how this script does not follow a straight baseline; instead it is drawn on a curve. The letters "F" and "s" will fall on approximately the same baseline. The top of the word "FOREVER" should follow the same curve. The bottom of "FOREVER" will sit on a straight baseline.

PRO TIP

When adding words that need to fit in a confined space, always count the letters and begin with the center letter. This will guarantee a centered word every time.

2 Since the key word is now securely in place, and our guidelines for the other words look correct and well balanced, we can feel confident about adding the other design elements. The words "LET'S BE" are contained within the space between the capital "F" and the "d" of "Friends."

3 Working from the top down, make multiple passes on each letter to polish and complete the outer shell of the shape, then fill them in.

4 Now that "LET'S BE" is darkened and developed, polish up the words "Friends" and "FOREVER" by thickening the downstrokes and drawing crisp edges.

Rest the side of your hand on the board to anchor it, much like we do when writing with a pencil or pen. To avoid the risk of smudging finished portions of your design, work from the top down.

5 Once you are happy with the letters, use a dry cotton swab to clean up any mistakes and erase your guidelines. I added simple, scratchy underlines for fun emphasis.

Congratulations! You've created a chalk art layout. Take out your smartphone, snap a photo, and send it to your bestie. Design a little off? No worries! Just erase and follow the steps again. You'll get the hang of it soon.

It's So Hard to Say Good-bye

I happily erase the drawings I am not quite fond of, but erasing something I am proud of is another story. I'm sure you, too, will experience that twinge of hesitation right as you reach for the eraser. It's sad! Unfortunately, unless you want chalkboards everywhere, there will come a time to say good-bye.

But, there is a solution! A photograph allows us to preserve an otherwise temporary and delicate art form. You don't need anything fancy. A simple point-and-shoot camera or even many smartphones can take photos with a high enough resolution to later print your design on a card or create a small print. Just place your design on a flat surface in even, natural light and take the photo from above. Be sure to take a few photos so you have plenty to choose from. Upload the photos to your computer and use photo-editing software to crop and resize to fit your needs. I like to change my artwork to "black and white" since sometimes a chalkboard will photograph with a blue tint. Voilà!

Part II
Taking Your
Designs to the
Next Level

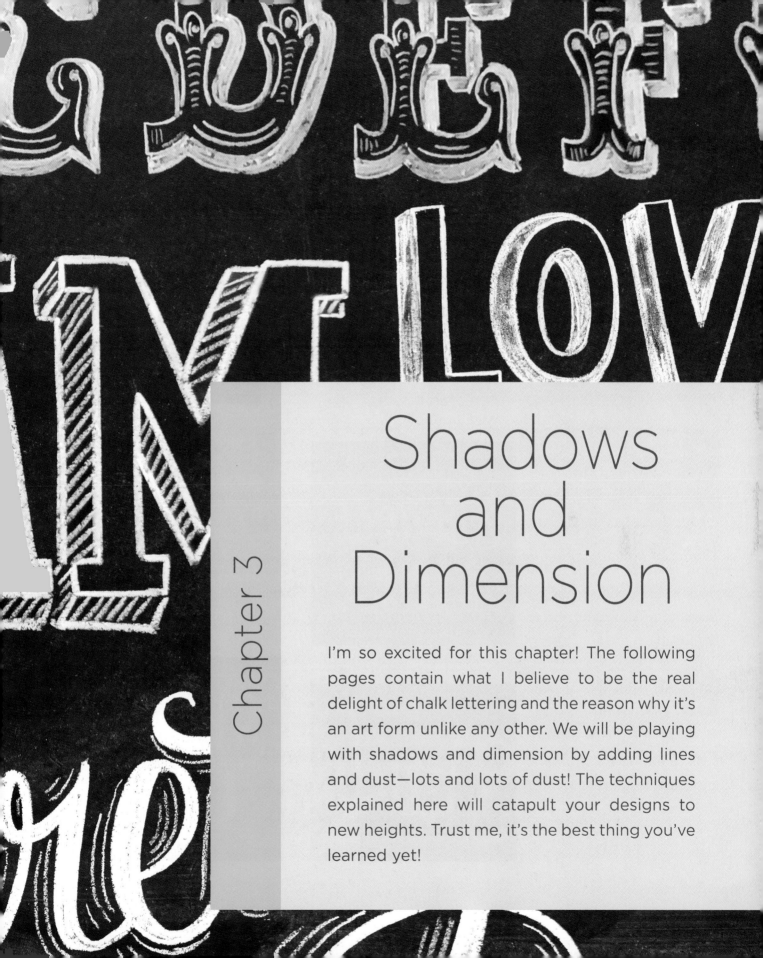

Shadows and Dimension

I'm so excited for this chapter! The following pages contain what I believe to be the real delight of chalk lettering and the reason why it's an art form unlike any other. We will be playing with shadows and dimension by adding lines and dust—lots and lots of dust! The techniques explained here will catapult your designs to new heights. Trust me, it's the best thing you've learned yet!

Adding Shadow Lines

Shadow lines can be added to all lettering styles. To determine their placement, first decide the direction of your light source. This isn't a real light source, but a way of perceiving shadows. Think of it this way: If the sun were hitting the right side of a house, the left side would be shadowed. Similarly, if the pretend light source were coming from the top right of the board, the bottom left side of the letters would have a shadow line.

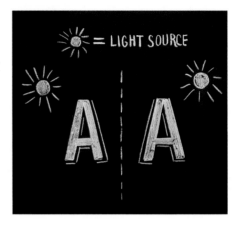

1 Start by drawing a phrase using two types of lettering styles and deciding on the light source. Here, let's have the light source come from the top left so the shadow lines will appear on the bottom and right side of the letters.

2 To add the shadow lines, follow the shape of each letter with a sharp chalk point on the appropriate side as if you are outlining the letter.

3 Now that the shadow lines on the right-hand side are completed, don't get too attached. Erase them with a cotton swab and add them on the opposite side. The next example's light source is coming from the top right, so the lines will be placed on the bottom and left side.

Kicking Shadow Lines Up a Notch

Shadow lines can be thick, thin, light, pronounced, tight to the letter, or farther away. Diagonal lines help achieve yet another dimensional look. This is one of my favorite effects!

1 Draw additional tiny, diagonal lines off the original line.

2 After adding the diagonal lines, go back over the original lines with a sharp point. This will help give a polished appearance to the final drawing.

Practice applying different amounts of pressure to develop understated or prominent shadow lines. Adding two or more shadow lines per letter as in the "Pretty" example is another way to achieve a totally different feel using the same technique.

Creating Soft Shadow Lines

Not all shadow lines need to be crisp. A softer edge might work better for your design. Let's practice with the phrase "HELLO THERE." We'll be using a serif style this time, but shadowing techniques apply to all types of lettering styles.

1 Create a wavy guideline. Draw two lines (top and bottom) to ensure a consistent wave.

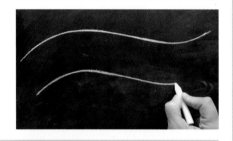

2 Draw the letters on the guideline. Then erase the line with a cotton swab. The shadow lines here are drawn very tight to the letters, which achieves a different result.

3 Let's take our "HELLO THERE" example even further. Using extremely light pressure, drag the chalk in short bursts, feathering out your original shadow line. The shadow line becomes much more muted and recessed compared to the vivid lettering.

4 Then, use a cotton swab to slightly clean up the edges for a more finished look. You don't want a crisp line here, just a soft, even edge.

Drawing Dimension

Once you are comfortable with shadow lines, you can use them to create dimension. The 3-D effect works well with block letters and is essentially created by expanding shadow lines.

1 Draw the word "LOVE" in a funky block style that has not been filled in, but is just the outline of the letters.

2 Keeping them evenly spaced, draw the shadow lines farther away from the letters this time.

3 Connect the lines to the letters at an angle to obtain the dimensional look.

4 Fill in the space you just drew with a blunt piece of chalk.

5 Use your finger to smudge the filled-in portions just a tiny bit. This extra, subtle texture really livens the whole word.

Overlapping Letters

For another take on the dimensional effect, draw the outline of the word "DREAM" in a serif style. In typography, this is called a slab serif because of the thick, blocklike serifs.

PRO TIP

Don't hesitate to turn your chalkboard to find a position that's best for you. Sometimes it may be easier to draw horizontally.

1 Draw the letters, leaving just a small bit of room between the characters.

2 Because of the spacing of the letters, the dimensional portion of the design will overlap at points. When portions of lettering meet in this way, do not connect the overlapped portion to the letter next to it. Leaving a tiny gap will create a look of dimension as opposed to one connected mass. Instead of filling the letters in, use a sharp chalk point to create short diagonal strokes within the areas you just drew.

3 Go back over the letter lines with a sharp edge to polish and finish the design.

Yay, Ombré!

Shading your letters is another way to manipulate dust for adding dimension. Who says a letter either needs to be entirely filled in or left empty? An ombré effect (meaning shaded or graduated in tone) works well, too!

1 Draw the word "YAY" in a block style.

2 Fill in the bottom of the letters. Use a heavy-handed pressure to create dust to work with and give vibrancy to the bottom portion.

3 Once you've filled the letters in about halfway up, use your finger to lift and carry the dust to the top portion of each letter until you have the desired ombré effect. If you take too much dust away, simply add more and try again. Likewise, if you've added too much dust, use your finger or cotton swab to take some away.

4 Clean up any smudges with a cotton swab, and redraw the letter outline to refine it.

Outlining Outlines

Outlining is another trick to build visual interest. Since the line is the same the whole way around the letter, there's no need to take the light source into consideration. You can also add dimension to the outline.

1 Using the "YAY" we just created with its textured effect, add a thin outline around all letters.

2 An additional dimensional effect can be added to the outlined word if you wish to continue its transformation.

3 Finally, I added an ombré effect to the dimensional portion of the letters for further interest. The possibilities are endless for manipulating letters and words using the same basic techniques!

Dust Is Your Friend

In its simplest form, chalkboard art is essentially adding and removing dust. Enhancing the background with dust is another way to create dimension.

1 Draw a simple, scribbled swirly border around your "YAY" design. Using an eraser, pat the outer surface of the board and swirl the dust around. This highlights the non-dusty portion contained within the swirly border.

2 Remove everything so just the ombré letters remain. A damp cotton swab will create a contrast of dust vs. no dust. Apply pressure to the cotton swab and drag it along the side of the letter as if you were drawing a shadow line.

3 Continue wiping away any dust as thick as you would like the "shadow" to appear. It will look exceptionally black when the water first touches the board, but it will dry to a lighter shade. You may need to keep going over the shadow with the wet cotton swab to remove all traces of dust.

4 You can try this same technique with a script style to make it pop!

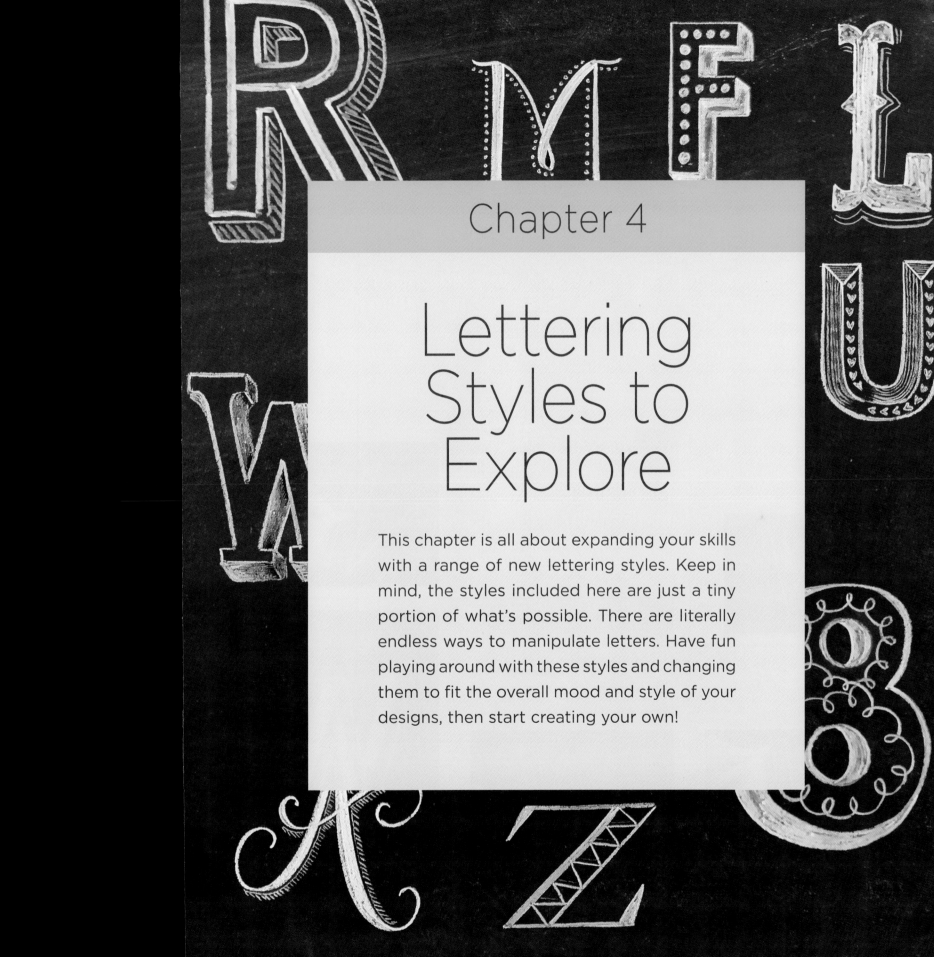

Chapter 4

Lettering Styles to Explore

This chapter is all about expanding your skills with a range of new lettering styles. Keep in mind, the styles included here are just a tiny portion of what's possible. There are literally endless ways to manipulate letters. Have fun playing around with these styles and changing them to fit the overall mood and style of your designs, then start creating your own!

Faceted Style

This style is meant to give the appearance of a chiseled letter with multiple cut edges. Its dimensional look reminds me of the letters you would see carved into stone or on an antique wooden sign.

Although it's a decorative lettering style, faceted style is extremely versatile since the end shape is contained within a sans serif block style. Faceted letters look lovely when used for emphasizing main words and paired with simpler serif and sans serif lettering.

1 Start with an open shape of a "W" drawn in a block format.

2 Next, draw triangles on each stem of the letter on the top and bottom.

3 Then, draw lines connecting the top triangle points to the bottom triangle points. You will begin to see the faceted nature of the letter take shape.

4 To better bring out the dimension of the letter, completely draw in the right side of each separation you just created.

5 The letter could be complete as it stands, but to give it further interest, lightly draw rough markings on the left sides and triangles. Use your fingers to blur the rough edge into a shadow.

6 Once the desired blurred appearance has been reached, polish the edges of the letter by going back over them with a sharp chalk point.

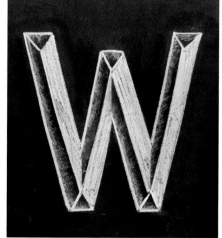

Vintage Circus Style

Elaborate lettering is so much fun to draw! This style is reminiscent of the type of lettering you would see on an old circus poster. It's heavily influenced by ornate turn-of-the-century type.

Use this style sparingly, on headlines and main words, to really make them stand out. I love pairing this style with contrasting, soft flourishes and wave banners, which will contribute to a late eighteenth- or early nineteenth-century inspired design.

1 Start with an open outline of an "L." Pay attention to the varied serifs and the interesting shape of the "leg" or bottom stroke.

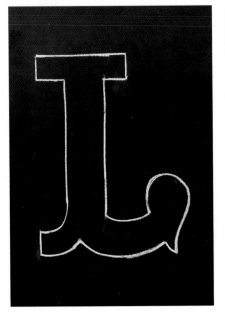

2 Add in a curved decoration on either side of the main body about halfway down the letter and erase the lines within the curvature.

3 Starting in the slab serif, draw horizontal lines not quite reaching the edge of the outline. Gradually, make the strokes less bold as you go down the letter to the center. Connect the curves with a half circle at the top and draw the details within the curved space.

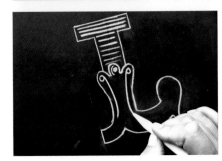

4 Continue adding thin, slightly curved lines the rest of the way down the stem and on the bottom serif, as well as decorative details on the leg.

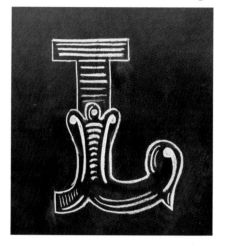

5 Chalk in an outline for a blocky, dimensional effect on the right and bottom sides of the letter.

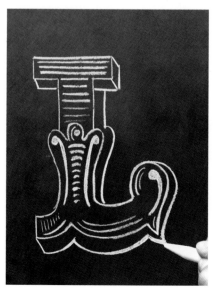

6 Fill this space in with a blunt piece of chalk. Smudge the chalk slightly to create a textured result.

Bubble Style

Bubble letters are chunky, bold, and playful, and a design containing them will immediately translate as such. This style is most often associated with graffiti (or middle school), but its roots come from lettering of the 1960s.

Bubble letters aren't very hard to draw since their rounded shape is forgiving and they are meant to look a bit uneven. Upper- and lowercase letters can be combined in the same word for a more casual feel. These cartoonish letters are impactful when used in fun designs for celebratory occasions.

1 When drawing the outline for the letters, keep the edges soft and rounded.

2 Roughly chalk inside and around the edges of the letters. Then, smudge the dust with your fingers to create a soft texture.

3 Alternate adding dust and smudging dust, until a smooth look with variants in the shading has been achieved. The light and dark spots will make the letters appear rounded instead of a flat look that would come from filling them in evenly.

PRO TIP

To highlight the big, easygoing nature of the bubble style, I stacked the letters so that the "B" is on top of the "I," and the "I" is on top of the "G." When you are shading elements that are stacked, keep a space close to the overlapping letter free of dust. This creates a subtle black divider that highlights each letter instead of turning the letters into one big blob.

Ribbon Style

As with most formal script letters, this style is calligraphic in nature. However, the benefit of drawing the lettering in chalk is that we can achieve a shaded effect. A few key-placed shadows transform the letters from a typical script to a cascading ribbon of chalk dust. This eye-catching, dimensional style can stand alone in a design, especially when paired with similarly shaded flourishes.

1 Roughly sketch the script "R" form, making sure you have two overlapping swirls. Our ribbon effect will really shine in those spots.

PRO TIP

The thin parts of the letter are the points where the ribbon would twist. For example, the ribbon comes off the leg of the "R," twists so that the "inside" of the ribbon is showing, and then twists again so the opposite side of the ribbon is exposed.

2 As you would with any variation of calligraphic-style script lettering, thicken the downstrokes of the letter.

3 Thicken the ends on the three entry and exit points of the "R" to look like the ends of a ribbon.

4 Fill in the thickened spaces with chalk, leaving small, chalk-free areas where the letter overlaps itself or comes out of a twist.

5 Using a combination of your finger and cotton swab, soften the edges and pull the chalk so it is graduated in intensity. The closer to the overlap it is, the darker it should be. Add slight texture to the downstrokes for visual interest.

6 Using pressure and a damp cotton swab, create a shadow on the right side of the strokes to complete the ribbon look.

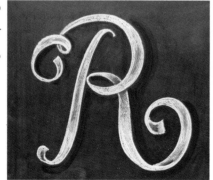

Spooky Style

Chalk art is enchanting for every season, but there's something particularly perfect about a chalkboard's darkness for Halloween! This spooky style is essentially the opposite of bubble lettering as it is created with straight lines to avoid any rounded edges. The hard pressure used to make the letter coupled with jagged, uneven markings, makes this simple style unsettling and undeniably hand-drawn. Use this style sparingly to add a hint of spookiness to keywords.

1 Draw the lettering to be pointed without any rounded edges.

PRO TIP

For letters that have a curve like "S," "P," and "O," think of the lettering as if you were creating them out of sticks. How would you place each straight piece to connect the letterforms? By using this simple technique, the design will feel scratchy and slightly sinister.

2 Go back over the lines, thickening portions of the letters to look like spikes. Use heavy pressure to create harsh, dramatic lines that aren't completely filled in.

3 Add shadow lines to give the letters more emphasis and readability.

4 A spooky word is made even creepier with chalk cobwebs. Use a lighter pressure and a sharp point when creating the cobweb lines. They are meant to appear soft compared with the vivid lettering.

Blackletter Style

Blackletter is sometimes referred to as Gothic script and it's easy to see why. This style, featuring angular lines instead of smooth curves, was widely used throughout Western Europe beginning around the twelfth century. The lettering looks medieval, because that's exactly what it is! Today, it is often used on diplomas or religious writings. Use this style for designs requiring a formal or solemn look. I think it would work especially well for both a Gothic-style Halloween design or a holiday card.

1 Draw a rough shape of a "P," enclosing the bowl of the letter with straight lines. Add an angled serif.

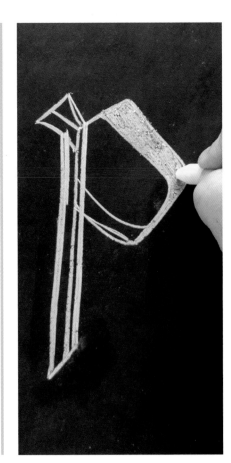

2 Thicken the top and bottom strokes of the bowl while leaving the connecting strokes thin for contrast.

3 Draw the serif into an angular shape and thicken the stem. It should come to an angled point at the bottom. Fill in the letter completely.

4 With a sharp chalk point, exaggerate the angles by drawing thin lines off the serif and the bottom of the stem. Add a curved decorative line to the left side of the stem.

Retro Style

This lettering style combines many of the skills you learned in Chapter 3 (pages 29–37). You could expect to see this outlined style in advertisements, posters, and other 1930s paper ephemera. Today, retro designs are anything but outdated. They are extremely popular especially when drawn on a chalkboard.

This style works just as well in designs with modern elements. Pair this retro lettering with a simple sans serif or block typeface for a coordinated look.

1 Draw a simple, thin "T" and add an outline around the whole letter with equal spacing.

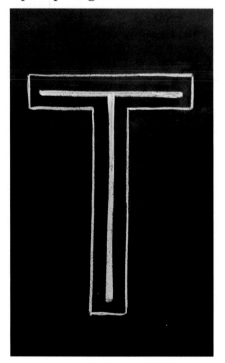

2 Draw another thin line very close to the outline. This is our shadow line. With a sharp point, draw short, evenly spaced, diagonal lines off the shadow line.

3 Instead of leaving the diagonal lines open, enclose them in another thin line, evening the diagonal lines as you draw.

ABCDEFG
HIJKLM
NOPQRST
UVWXYZ
1234567890

Western Style

Characterized by distinct serifs, this lettering style is immediately recognizable as belonging to the American Wild West period of the 1800s. However, it is much more versatile than you think. When used in small doses, Western lettering adds an antique nod and interest to casual designs—not to mention a little rustic-chic. It can be used as headlines or secondary words, and looks particularly great with complementary letters, such as simple thin serifs with vintage flourishes.

1 Draw a rough, basic "H" shape.

2 Add heavy, winged serifs to both the top and bottom of the letter and fill in the shape.

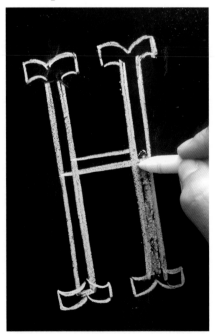

3 Add small triangles to the crossbar of the "H." This small embellishment completely changes the feel of the letter.

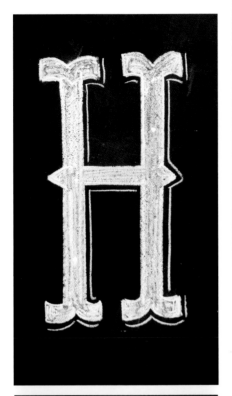

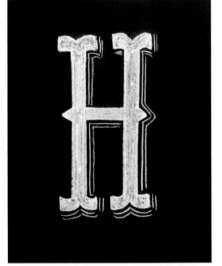

ABCDEFG
HIJKLM
NOPQRST
UVWXYZ
1234567890

Whimsical Serif Style

As with Western-style lettering, the charm of this style is created mostly by serifs. The shape of this whimsical serif is reminiscent of turn-of-the-century hand-lettering, but it's made modern with the addition of a designed strip through the letter.

Use this style on keywords in your designs. Supplement the main text with secondary words drawn in the same style but without the mid strip. Flourishes that follow the same shape as the serif offer a nice repetition for overall cohesiveness.

1 Draw the "Y" with an exaggerated thickness on the downstroke side.

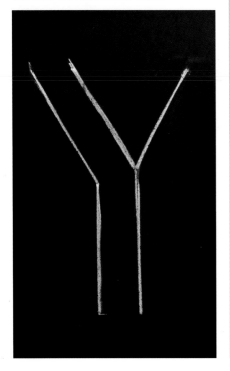

2 Add serifs, this time drawing them in an "S" shape so they are wavy and curled on the ends.

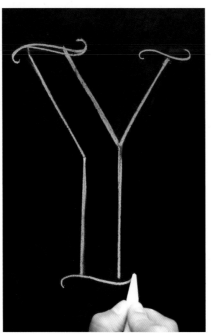

3 Fill in the downstroke of the "Y," leaving a strip in the center untouched.

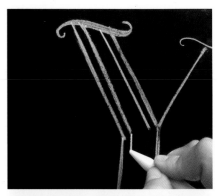

4 I decided to draw a thin line with a few cute dots in the center, but you could fill it in with dots or even tiny hearts the whole way down. The possibilities are endless!

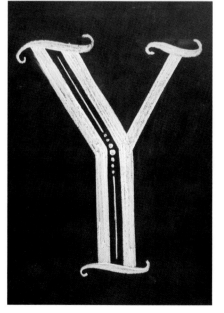

A B C D E F G
H I J K L M
N O P Q R S T
U V W X Y Z
1 2 3 4 5 6 7 8 9 0

Cute Style

Script lettering can look elegant, but also playful and, well, cute. I like to use it on an angled baseline to create a 1950s look.

This script works well for adding sweetness and whimsy to designs without being overly formal. It is versatile for both headlines and secondary words.

1 Using lowercase letters, draw the word "cute." Add a long, curved crossbar to your "t" and embellish the ends with circles. Embellish the ends of the "c" and the "e" as well.

2 Draw heavy downstrokes on the letters and fill in completely.

3 Finish with shadow lines.

Classic Style

This polished style is timeless and gives the appearance of dimension. Since it is a subtle, traditional look, it can be used in many different ways and in designs with various moods.

Although it's based on Roman letterforms, this sophisticated style is anything but stale.

1 Start with a classic "O" shape and thicken both sides leaving the top and bottom thin.

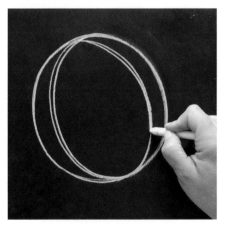

2 Fill in the letter with a blunt piece of chalk.

3 Using a cotton swab, remove a strip of chalk, following the curve of the "O" close to the farthest left side. Continue removing chalk until you have a curved shape that opens thinly at the top, gradually gets thicker, and then thins again at the end point. Do the same thing to the right side.

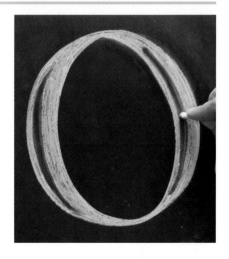

Chapter 5

Banners, Borders, and Frames

Banners, borders, and frames go hand in hand with chalk art. From simple to ornate, these core elements are found on chalkboards everywhere, making hand-lettering stand out and shine. Starting with the most basic shapes, we will move forward, step-by-step, into fun variations full of character and charm.

The Basic Banner

1 Start with a rectangle. Use a straightedge to draw two long, horizontal lines and then connect them to form a box.

2 About a quarter of the way down the right side, freehand draw the wings of the banner. I like drawing the wings to look like a triangle has been cut out of them.

3 Now, connect the wing to the bottom corner of the rectangle with a small triangle.

4 Repeat Steps 2 and 3 on the left side.

5 Shade the triangles you just drew and add subtle lines on the wings. This will make them appear as if they are shadowed and add emphasis to the main portion of the banner.

The Curved Banner

1 Instead of two horizontal lines, begin with two curved lines. It may take a few tries to draw them evenly.

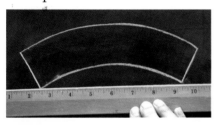

2 Use a straightedge to make sure the points line up.

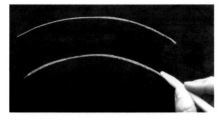

3 Draw the wings and attach each to the banner with a triangle.

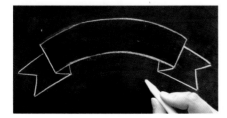

4 Fill in the wings, smudging the space where they touch the main body of the banner. This creates a shadow, which adds to the banner appearing as though it is folded on itself.

5 To take it a step further, fill in the main body of the banner as well. Smudge the chalk so that it is filled in, but not completely solid. Add any lettering to the banner with a heavy pressure. You want the word to look vibrant compared to the dulled chalk background.

6 Use a cotton swab to remove the chalk immediately surrounding the letters, following the principles of a shadow. The word "CURVE" will now stand out and appear dimensional.

The Stacked Banner

1 A stacked banner is created by first drawing two or more rectangles on top of each other, leaving some space between each one. For this example, I drew two rectangles using a straightedge on a diagonal, but they could also be straight.

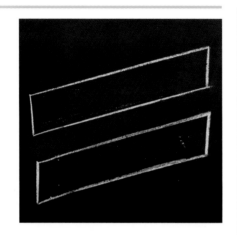

2 Connect the two rectangles with two diagonal lines. The middle lines will form the "inside" of the banner, as if it were being folded. (It is helpful to think of it this way especially when it's time to add shading.) The width of all three pieces should be similar.

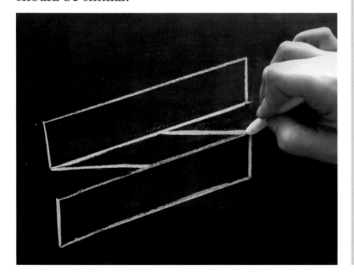

3 To insert the ends of the banner, draw two more diagonal lines shooting from the top right and bottom left corners. Don't forget to add the cut-out triangle shape.

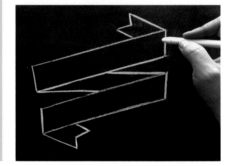

4 Completely fill in the banner's middle and top and bottom ends.

The Wave Banner

The wave banner is my favorite to use. It is so versatile and whimsical!

1 Start with two wavy lines. The top line should curve upwards on the left side. The bottom line should curve downward on the right side. On both sides, draw a line connecting the bottom and top curve.

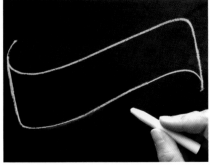

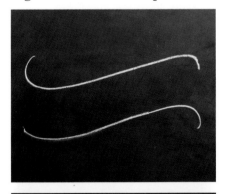

2 Extend the curve on the right side toward the middle of the banner until it almost touches, then loop it around to come back toward the end of the banner.

3 Extend the line to create the banner's wing and add another line above it following the same curve.

4 Be sure the tail has a similar width to the main body of the banner and enclose the lines with a cut-out triangle shape. Repeat on the left side.

5 Connect the "looped" portion of the banner to the main body with a small, straight line.

6 Add dimension by shading in the loop. I used tight, straight lines.

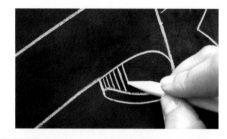

7 Add soft shading to the wings, sides, and body of the banner to create the appearance of a rounded shape.

8 Smudge them with your finger in a sweeping motion for a subdued look.

The Double Wave Banner

You can add as many folds as you like using this method. It works well when you have two or more words to enclose.

1 Start as if you are making a wave banner, but draw a shorter body.

2 When you bring your loop back around, instead of finishing it as a tail, extend it with a curve to create another banner shape.

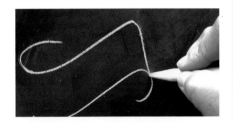

3 Add the top line to this new banner following the curve and starting at the appropriate height to create a similar banner thickness. Close up the end.

4 Now that you have an extra "fold" in the center of the banner, finish the end with a tail.

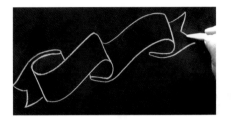

5 Finish the form by shading and smudging the looped areas and tails. Smudge them with your finger in a sweeping motion for a subdued look.

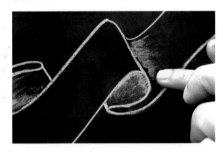

6 Add curved shadowing to the banner coming out of the centerfold.

The Cascading Ribbon Banner

1 Begin with three sets of wave banner lines and finish with a small tail. (I drew these to decrease in length with each banner.) Be conscious of the space between the banners.

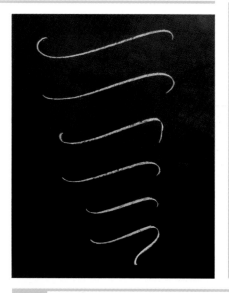

2 Enclose the sides of each banner with straight lines.

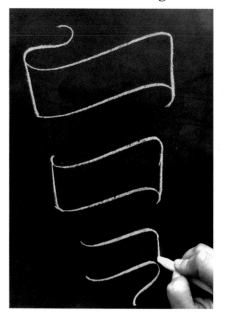

3 Connect the three banners by pulling the curved ends to the middle points (or close to the middle points) of the banner below and above it. The connecting strips should be of similar thickness.

4 To create the top tail of the banner, close the loop with a straight line connecting to the main body. Add another line to close the smaller loop above it.

5 Use shading to bring out the look of the newly created bends.

6 Add shading to the connecting portions of the banner to complete the realistic ribbon appearance.

7 Smudge them with your finger in a sweeping motion.

This flowing banner will look like a piece of ribbon delicately falling.

Picture Perfect
Frames and Borders

Just as a picture frame enhances the art inside, a drawn frame or border is meant to do the same. These techniques offer yet another fun element to add to your growing collection of design strategies.

Basic Polka Dot Border

1 Measure and mark all four corners of the board. Connect these markings with a straightedge.

2 In freehand, go over the lines to achieve the desired thickness. This requires a steady hand to keep the line straight, but still keep that imperfect, hand-drawn look.

3 Now that you have a thick outer border, use a sharp piece of chalk to draw a thin inner border. The space between the original border and the second border should leave enough space for a tiny string of polka dots. Be aware of the spacing so that it is as evenly spaced as possible the whole way around.

4 Once the secondary line is drawn, add tiny polka dots in the space between the thick outer border and the thin inner border. The polka dots give this simple border a sweet look.

Elaborate Cornered Frame

4 Fill in that space with a drawn element. Simple embellishments, like starburst lines, will work well. Remember, the border is meant to complement what's inside.

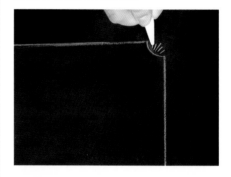

1 Once the basic border is formed, measure from the center of each corner (here I used a ½ inch) and place a dot.

3 Erase the sharp corner leaving the half-circle space empty.

5 Elaborate the design even further by adding a repeating starburst on the opposite side of the half circle and adding a double border.

2 Connect the corners with a half circle passing through the mark you drew.

The possibilities for corner decorations are endless! Here are just a few other ideas.

Vine Leaf Border

1 Start by placing carelessly straight lines within the chalk grid.

2 Add little leaf outlines and swirls to the lines.

3 Complete the border by erasing the corner marks and inserting a little flower, swirls, or additional leaves.

A border edge does not always have to be straight. A vine leaf border is a cute way to achieve a loose, quirky look for your design.

Antique Oval Frame

1 Mark the center points from top to bottom and side to side where you want the oval to be placed.

2 Then, mark the center points between the dots you just drew and connect them with a curved line.

3 Once you are happy with the oval, follow the shape to draw two smaller ovals inside it. These layers will help achieve the look of an antique frame. The lines can be coarsely chalked in. We will go back over them with shading.

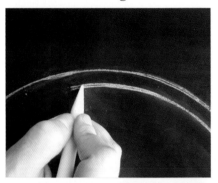

PRO TIP

Don't be discouraged if your oval doesn't look right the first time. It will likely take a few passes. I am constantly tweaking and drawing over my ovals until the dimension looks correct.

4 Think of this frame as having three chiseled ridges. Each line represents a new layer. Using either chalk, your finger, or a cotton swab (or a combination of all three), shade in each line. The intensity of your shading should decrease the closer you get to the most inner line, where the frame would theoretically dip in. The outer line should be the brightest of the three.

5 Add circles all around the third layer.

6 Roughly mark one side of the circles with a piece of chalk and smudge the mark to give the appearance of rounded dimension.

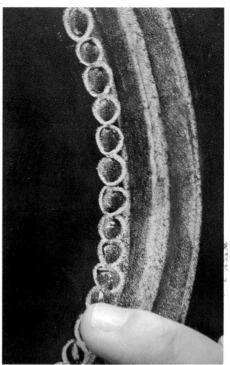

This frame style is feminine and pretty with simple chalk shading.

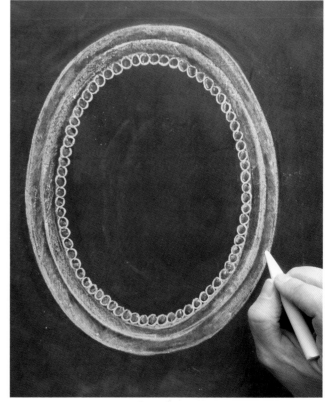

Ornate Oval Frame

1 Draw a basic oval shape and draw "S"-shaped swirls around the perimeter.

2 Vary the "S" shapes by adding a few swirls here and there and making the shapes a bit different each time.

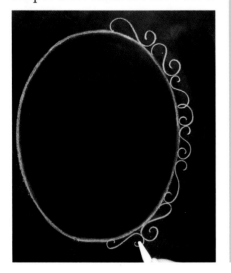

3 Once the initial layer is drawn, go back through and add small swirls protruding from the centers of the "S" shapes.

4 To up the vintage factor, add tiny circle endings to each swirl.

Oval and Rectangle Frame

1 Measure from the corners of a basic border line and draw a diagonal line. I used 1 inch.

2 Using a straightedge, connect these lines, producing the look of a traditional picture frame.

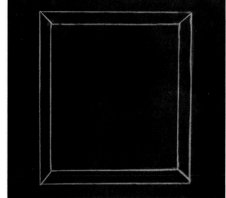

3 Next, draw an oval shape within the frame. The oval will be the frame opening. I fancied it up by adding a cute scalloped border around the edges.

4 Fill in the frame with chalk and soften with your finger.

5 Decrease the intensity of the shading on the side panels at the points where they touch another panel. This will create a "ridge."

6 Intensify all the borders by going over them with heavy pressure.

7 To add further interest, draw swirls in the corners and use a cotton swab to erase a heart shape.

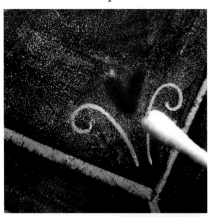

I couldn't resist adding lettering into the oval. It's just so lovely! The frame makes the words come alive.

9 Since this design looks so much like a real picture frame, I added a drawn hanger.

8 Using a sharp point, draw a heart-shaped border around this silhouette.

Funky Frame

1 Use your imagination to create a funky frame shape. I used a rectangle opening with a straightedge, but this could be left out.

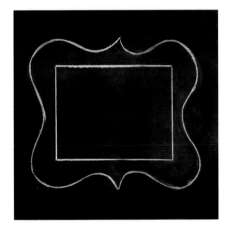

Banners and borders work well separately, but practice pairing them in the same design. They make a lovely couple, don't you think?

2 Thicken the outer border by lightly filling it in while leaving the outlines vibrant. Thicken the inside border using heavy pressure to create contrast.

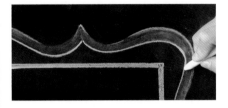

Don't just think of borders and frames in terms of squares or circles —borders come in all shapes.

3 Connect the outer and inner borders by drawing thin lines in a starburst form.

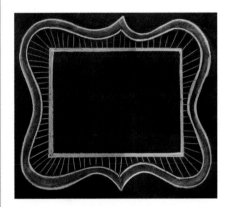

BORDERS AND BANNERS work well TOGETHER IN DESIGN

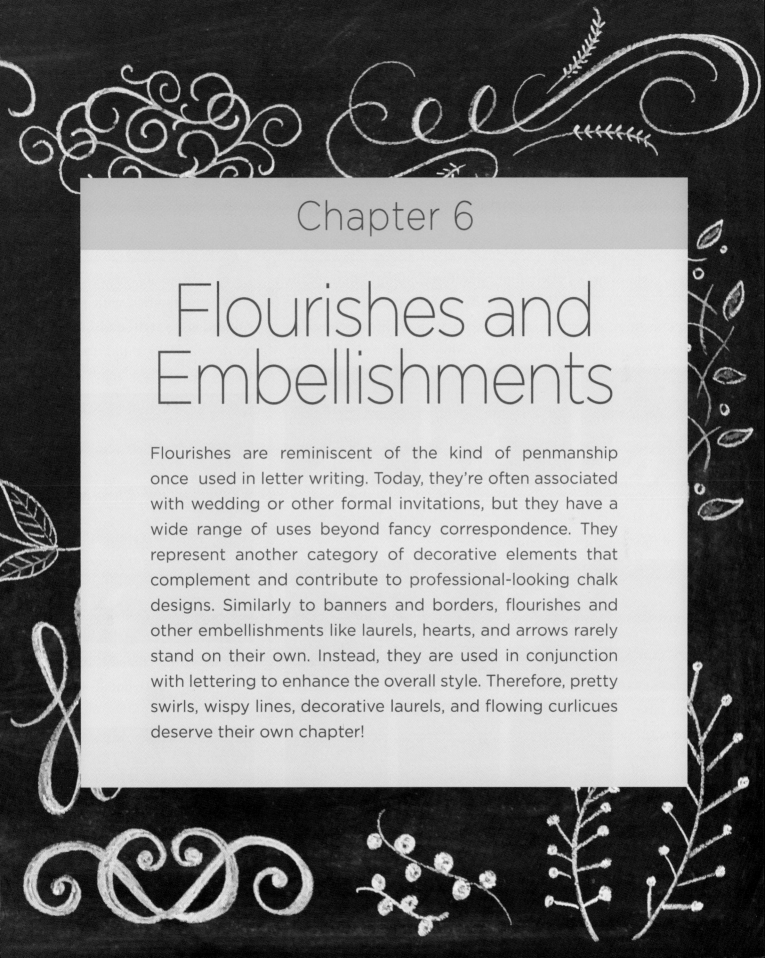

Chapter 6

Flourishes and Embellishments

Flourishes are reminiscent of the kind of penmanship once used in letter writing. Today, they're often associated with wedding or other formal invitations, but they have a wide range of uses beyond fancy correspondence. They represent another category of decorative elements that complement and contribute to professional-looking chalk designs. Similarly to banners and borders, flourishes and other embellishments like laurels, hearts, and arrows rarely stand on their own. Instead, they are used in conjunction with lettering to enhance the overall style. Therefore, pretty swirls, wispy lines, decorative laurels, and flowing curlicues deserve their own chapter!

Signature Flourish

Some form of this embellishment seems to find its way into most of my chalk designs. It's uncomplicated at its core, but the end result is fanciful and lovely.

1 Draw a series of alternating, side-to-side loops to create the main shape. Think of the motion as making a series of figure eights. Drawing the outline in one swoop without lifting the chalk from the board produces the most natural-looking, smooth end result.

2 Although it could stand as is, thickening the bottom strokes of the loop gives it a polished finish.

Use this same technique to create a variety of curly options.

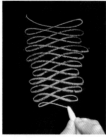  

Tight   Loose   Overlapping

3 For a fun twist, finish the flourish with a few spiraled loops at the end. I think these spirals look like curling ribbon or party streamers.

The signature flourish works well both horizontally and vertically.

Wispy Flourish

Simple lines drawn with a sense of motion create wispy, effortless embellishments.

1   Start with a main centerline, then draw lines with differing lengths above and below it.

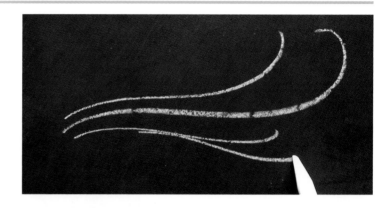

2   Use the main line as a guide for the shape of subsequent lines. In this example, each line decreased in length as I stacked them. I also thickened my main line while leaving the other lines thin.

3   Add a few strings of tiny polka dots to bring a sweet touch.

Spiral and Wisp Flourish

This simple flourish combines a horizontal spiral overlapped on simple wispy lines. It works perfectly as an underline.

1 Draw a slightly curved main line.

2 Add thin, wispy lines on the top and bottom of the right side of the main line. Some wisps should follow the curve of the main line while others can break away from the curve.

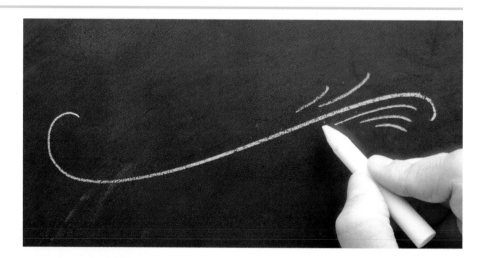

3 Draw a series of spirals on top of the main line starting on the left side so that it looks as though this line is going through the spirals.

4 Thicken one side of the spiral loops for interest.

Ornate Flourish

Ornate flourishes may appear daunting to draw at first. However, when broken down, these fancy swirls are actually quite simple.

1 Start with the basic wavy shape, but emphasize the swirl on one end.

2 Build on this main swirl by adding smaller swirls that follow the same curvature.

3 Create detail and depth by drawing a few thin lines off-shooting from the original swirls.

4 Add thicker embellishments that also follow the same curves, like a leaf-shaped element, to create a sense of dimension.

5 Look for empty spaces to fill in. Continue adding lines and curls to fill gaps or connect to already existing swirls.

6 The point where your curves make a "V" is a great place to insert another line or shape. Ornate flourishes are created in these tiny details. Mix things up by thickening certain lines and leaving others thin.

Heavy Flourish

A flourish can be delicate and light, but it can also be bold and heavy.

1 Start with the familiar "S" shape drawn as mirror images of each other.

2 Finish the ending points with circles to add visual weight. Draw smaller, curled hook shapes off the main shape.

3 Thicken all of the original lines.

4 Following the curve shape, add thick wing-shaped details to each side.

5 Fill in the "V"-shaped gap where the two original "S" shapes meet with an outline of a funky, pointed center shape.

6 Fill the other empty spaces by drawing smaller strokes with bulbs on the ends. Teardrop shapes on the center top and bottom complete the ornament.

Crisscross Flourish

A crisscross flourish offers the perfect shape to complete the bottom of your designs. It can be simple or complex with the addition of a few decorative elements.

1 Draw two overlapping lines to create an "X" shape with curled ends.

2 Bring one side down into a loop.

3 Mimic the shape on the opposite side and cross the lines again. A diamond shape will form in the center.

4 Turn these connecting strokes into another loop that faces downward.

5 Thicken the downstrokes.

6 Want a more formal look? Add further decorative elements and shadow lines.

Overlapping Wispy Flourish

This flourish is characterized by a combination of wispy lines and loops overlapping each other. To do this successfully, make sure enough of the curl overlaps. If the point of intersection only clips the end slightly, the overall look might appear unintentional.

1 Start with a main curved line, this time adding a small loop at the end.

2 Draw two lines under the main line following its curve.

3 Once you are happy with the placement of the secondary lines, extend the top line into a curve that intersects the main line. Shoot for the main line to intersect at the center point of the newly formed "C"-shaped curve.

4 Combine the lines into a cohesive flourish even further by drawing a "C"-shaped line through all three of the existing lines.

5 Extend the "C" shape into a loop almost mirroring the original loop in the main line and exit with a thin stroke curving upward.

6 Thicken and polish the lines to complete the final flourish.

Embellishing Letters

One of my favorite techniques involves adding embellishments to letters. This works best with script styles. Look for the points in your lettering that can expand into a lovely flourish without hurting the readability. This design is chock full of examples of letter extensions ripe for a little flourishing.

Flourishing can be extravagant or simplified. A simple, single swirled line can be a key addition to a streamlined design.

The more lines that are added, the more ornate the end result will be.

By alternating from thick to thin lines the flourish comes alive, evoking unwinding ribbons.

just a little Note

Crossbars are excellent opportunities to use flourishes. Inject your style and personality by playing with new shapes and swirls.

Use flourishes to balance out empty spaces and emphasize certain words.

A vintage flourish here adds shape and completes the composition with a dash of visual flair.

Laurels

You may be familiar with the image of ancient Greeks wearing a laurel wreath on their heads to signify victory. For our purposes, drawn laurels are excellent decorative elements to use in your chalk designs.

1 A laurel begins like most other flourishes with a wavy line. This creates the stem or the branch.

2 Add small, leaf-shaped outlines on both sides of the line.

3 Thicken one side of the leaf outlines to add dimension. The same side can be thickened on all leaves or you can vary which side to thicken. Either way, it creates a subtly defined end result.

Arrows and Hearts

Straight lines, whether underlines or starbursts, can draw attention to certain words in a design or create balance. And with a few additional strokes, straight lines can be transformed into arrows. Of course, hearts often go hand in hand with arrows. Employ these details when your designs need a little cuteness.

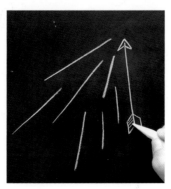

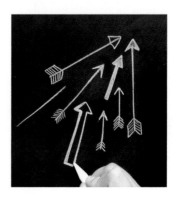

Chapter 7

Lettering in a Shape

It's one thing to letter inside a border or frame. But it's a whole other thing to form your letters into an actual shape. Manipulating letters in this way produces unique looks that are more about the whole design than each individual piece of lettering. When creating distinctively shaped layouts, think of it like a puzzle. The key is finding the right pieces! It's a challenge, but it's incredibly exciting when everything fits just right.

The Shape of My Heart
Heart-Shaped Lettering

In a later chapter, we'll draw a heart-shaped laurel containing words within it. For this project, we will also use a heart, but the words will create the actual heart shape.

1 Begin with a sketched heart.

2 Starting in the upper left portion of the heart, draw a "Y" with exaggerated strokes to make up the curve of the heart.

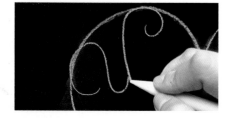

3 Continue with the "Y" descender, dragging it to follow another curve of the heart outline. Add an "o" and "u" to fill the space nicely. The exit stroke of the "u" should hit slightly above the dip in the center of the heart.

PRO TIP
The outline does not need to be too polished or perfect. Eventually, most of it will be covered with a combination of lettering and flourishes. Any remaining outline will be erased.

4 A key component of a heart is the dip in the center. It's important to exaggerate it with a drawn element so it stands out. Draw a flourish that outlines this depression.

5 On the other side of the heart, add a large "S" and an "O."

6 Move to the middle of the heart and add a flourish that will contain the word "ARE" above it and the word "Loved" below it. When drawing the "L" in "Loved" connect it to the outline in two places to help give shape to the heart.

7 Extend the exit point of the "L" into a signature flourish that will complete the heart's bottom point, another key area to emphasize. Once the words belonging on the edges of the heart fit nicely, add the word "ARE" above the center flourish line.

8 Look for any holes in the design. Does the empty spot under the word "So" and the space between the body of the "Y" and its descender look sparse?

9 Fill in these spaces with little hearts for a cute embellishment.

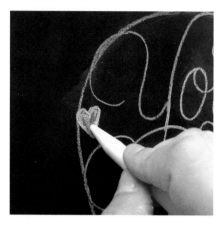

10 Once your design appears balanced and the outline looks significantly covered, use a cotton swab to erase any of the remaining heart-shaped outline.

11 From the top down, polish the letterforms by thickening the downstrokes and emphasizing the strokes forming the heart.

12 Add any shadow lines and flourishes to fill any holes that pop up.

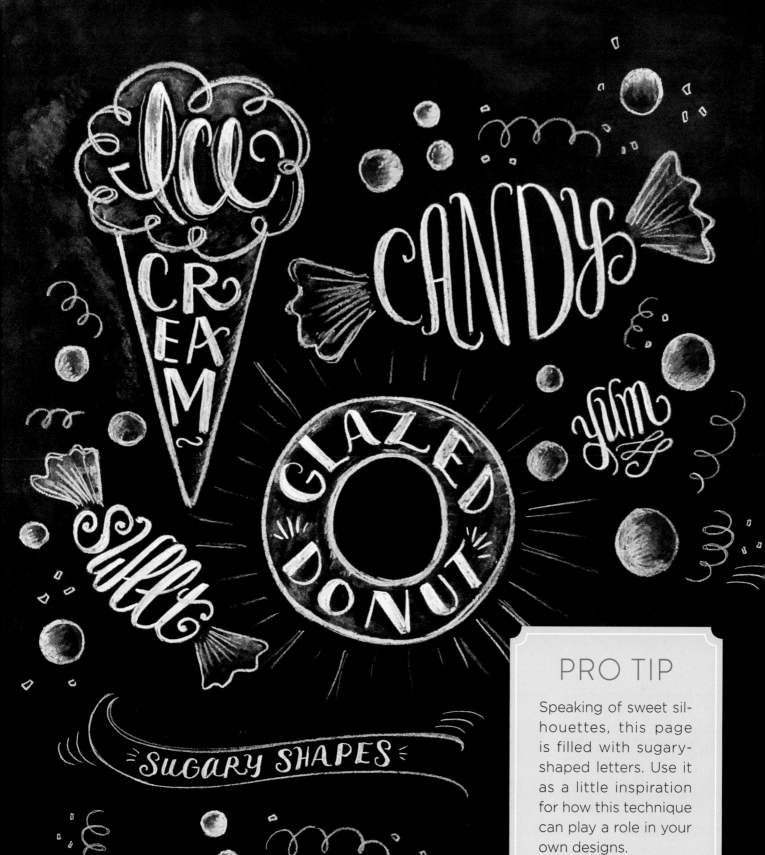

ICE CREAM

CANDY

GLAZED DONUT

yum

SWEET

SUGARY SHAPES

PRO TIP

Speaking of sweet sil-houettes, this page is filled with sugary-shaped letters. Use it as a little inspiration for how this technique can play a role in your own designs.

Monograms
Circular Lettering

Shaping techniques can be applied to other figures, like a simple but striking monogram.

1 Begin with a traced drawn circle.

PRO TIP

It's best to have a near perfect circle so I traced a circular object to make sure it was even.

2 Using a three-letter monogram, draw the center letter first. Once the first letter is positioned correctly, move to the other two. The outer letters are responsible for forming the circle shape. The leg of the "M" facing the center should remain straight, while the leg on the outside should be drawn on the same curve as the circle. The same holds true for the "V."

3 Polish the letters. For a bold, modern look thicken the letterforms evenly and add texture by removing some of the chalk inside. Use a cotton swab to erase the circle if you wish.

Fancy Monograms
Circular Lettering

For this monogram, the center letter will be the largest and most pronounced in the design. The other two letters will overlap and weave through it.

1 Trace a circle with the center letter "S" drawn as the starting point.

PRO TIP

The goal is to give the impression that the side letters are sitting behind the center letter. This makes the monogram feel like a unified piece. Having the tiny break in between intersection points achieves the look.

3 Add the "W." It should cross the body of the "S," and its right side should follow the curve of the circle. Thicken the downstrokes on all three letters.

2 Add the "L." The entry stroke of the "L" should follow the curve of the circle. Draw its exit stroke through the "S," without actually drawing a solid line through the letter.

4 Dab a cotton swab on the overlap points to add a subtle shadow and some dimension.

Here's the same technique used with different letters. Both the top and bottom portions of the "J" will intersect the "B" as well as the stem of the "R."

This time, I decided to bring the "J" forward. However, the serif of the "J" will continue to sit behind the "B" giving an intertwined look to the finished monogram.

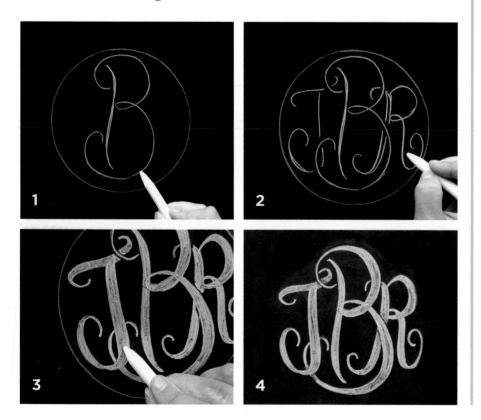

Here is yet another example of a three-letter script monogram. Although it looks beautiful on its own, remove the dust with a damp cotton swab for an irresistible dimension.

A heart also makes a lovely backdrop for a monogram shape and can work with many different lettering styles.

Hometown Pride
Random-Shape Lettering

A random shape, like that of one of the fifty states, provides a real challenge to letter inside. The act of drawing the outline of your home state alone is excellent practice in gaining freehand precision. Since my home state is Pennsylvania, I started there.

1 Draw the outline of the state (or shape).

2 Roughly sketch in the words to fill the space as completely as possible.

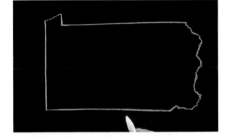

3 Polish and thicken the letters.

4 Add details, like wispy lines, to fill design holes.

5 Use embellishments, like hearts and arrows, to fill any awkward spaces in these designs. The uneven shapes of states give plenty of opportunities for creative flourishing in the gaps.

Chapter 8

Chalk Illustrations

We have focused mostly on lettering and the elements that enhance lettering. But another way to add depth and complexity to your designs is through basic illustrations. In this chapter, we will go through step-by-step lessons for illustrating two common items: flowers and snowflakes. The methods you're about to learn can be easily used to create all different types of illustrations. As with chalk lettering, illustrations are born out of a combination of adding chalk, smudging chalk, and removing chalk. That's it!

Chalk Flowers

Chalk flowers are one of my favorite things to draw and include in my designs. Illustrated blooms look particularly lovely when paired with laurel flourishes.

Since real petals are varied and interesting, allow nature to inspire your floral illustrating. Embrace the imperfection!

Daisies

A daisy-style flower illustration is made up of a circular center with petals all around it. This shape can be manipulated into endless forms and it's simple to create.

1 First, start with a circle center.

2 Attach petals around the circular center. The petal shape should be thin at the top and bottom but wider in the middle, resembling bunny ears.

3 Shade the center of the daisy and add subtle dots for detail.

Don't worry if each petal isn't exactly the same. The variety will give the flower personality.

4 With light pressure, draw soft lines at the base of each petal for interest. Draw a stem and leaf if desired.

Whimsical Daisies

Minor changes can be made to the basic daisy design to completely change the look.

1 Start with a circle center.

2 Instead of drawing precise petals, draw looped, tight petals.

3 Draw a soft line through each petal to add interest.

4 Instead of drawing a leaf on a stem, draw the leaf coming off the flower.

Tulips

Tulips are perfect for your spring designs. As with every flower, there are many ways to draw a tulip, but the basic shape stays the same.

1 Draw a horseshoe shape or a "U" with strokes that curve in at the top.

2 Draw an almond shape, similar to the daisy petals, in the center of the "U" you just drew.

3 Close the two outside ends by connecting them to the center shape with an angled line forming three triangles at the top.

4 Add a curved line connecting the two outside petals. This will provide the look of petals peeking out from the back of the flower.

5 Shade each individual petal for depth and dimension. Add a stem and long leaves with soft shading.

Playful Tulips

With the basic shape of a tulip, we can create a quirky flower that would be perfect for playful designs. I also like using this flower shape for decorating border corners.

1 Start with a "U" shape, but instead of curving inward, curve the strokes outward.

2 Connect the "U" with two "petals" on the ends and three triangle shapes in the middle.

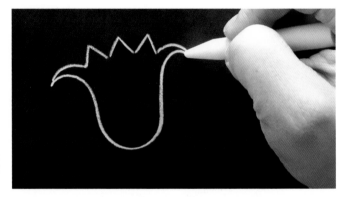

3 Draw simple stamens coming out of the flower and add shading to the base with drawn lines at the bottom. Finish this fun look with a stem, leaves, curly vines, and dots.

Open Roses

Chalk roses are born through shading soft, overlapping petals. They can be drawn many ways.

1 Begin with a tiny circle looped into a swirl.

2 Add small, tight curves to the swirl and build out. Keep the starting and ending points varied so the petals appear stacked. The petals should also increase in size the farther you go out and develop a wavy, uneven look.

3 Add chalk texture. The ends of the petals are the most exposed to light, therefore they will be bright white. As they get closer to the center, they will sink in a bit. Smudge your chalk with this in mind.

4 Go back through with a sharp piece of chalk and emphasize the petals with drawn lines. Add a leaf or two if desired.

Partially Open Roses

The partially open rose begins in a similar way as the open rose, but the beginning swirl is thicker.

1 Pretend as though you are wrapping this original swirl in two flourishes—one coming from the left and one from the right.

2 Connect both sides by drawing the body of the rose. To give the appearance of a partially open rose, draw small petals on the body.

3 Smudge chalk on the petals, leaving dark spots in between the layers.

4 Because of the perspective of this rose, it looks best with a drawn stem and leaves.

A closed bud is created with just a slight variation. The additional petals are not added to the body—all of the petals face upward.

Drawing a lily is great practice since it too can morph into many different types of flower drawings.

1 Sketch large, irregularly shaped petals with some of the petals coming from underneath the others.

2 Emphasize the centerlines of the petals and add lots of dust to smudge. Leave the center of the lily, where the petals converge, without dust.

3 Use a sharp point and heavy pressure to draw the stamens originating from the center. Wipe away chalk as needed.

4 If desired, add irregular spots to the petals to mimic a stargazer or tiger lily.

Dot Flowers

Dot flowers aren't necessarily inspired by an actual flower, but they'll bring a charming texture to your designs. I love combining this style with other floral illustrations for an end result full of interest and variety.

1 Draw one center circle surrounded by five similarly shaped circles.

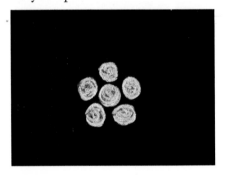

  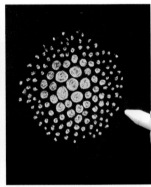

2 Working from the center out, draw circles all around these original five. The dots should get smaller the farther they are from the center. Continue adding dots as they look good to you. The outermost dots should be quite small. Vary the edge of the outer dots—a perfect circle is not necessary.

3 Add a stem and leaf. Just as you would vary the flower illustrations in a design, alter the size and shape of the leaves and stems as well.

Chalk Snowflakes

Snowflakes can be the main focus of your winter designs or used as tiny embellishments for interest and balance. The beauty of hand-drawn snowflakes is that no two will ever be the same —just like in nature.

Simple Snowflakes

A basic snowflake shape is comprised of six points or three lines converging together.

1 Draw an "X" shape, then draw one more line through the "X." Thicken these lines as desired.

2 Add six tiny off-shooting lines to each main line to create a very simple snowflake.

3 Draw triangles between each main line in the center to connect them.

Thick Snowflakes

Now, let's take this main concept and draw it in a different, bolder way.

1 Instead of thin main lines, create thick lines that come to a point on the ends. Add two off-shooting lines at each point, making these thick as well.

2 Connect the lines in the center with triangles as we did before, but this time, lightly fill in the space and draw thin lines branching off of each triangle point.

3 Continue adding intricacies by drawing tiny off-shooting lines in the center and another connecting string of triangles.

Elegant Snowflakes

This technique for drawing snowflakes relies
on different sized circles.

1 Draw centerlines and connect them with half-circle shapes.

2 Erase the lines in between your half circles and add embellishments. On the main lines of the snowflake, draw three circles that decrease in size as they get closer to the points.

3 Add diamond-shaped offshoots between each main line and draw branches on the six points.

Dot Snowflakes

A snowflake comprised completely of dots is another take on an elegant snowflake.

1 Draw a basic "asterisk" snowflake shape and draw a dot in the center.

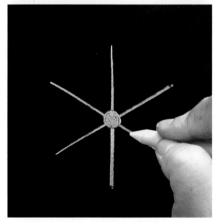

2 Starting closest to the center, draw a series of dots decreasing in size on each off-shooting line and fill in the dots.

3 Draw tiny dots in a line between each main string of dots.

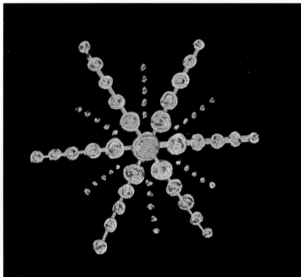

Outline Snowflakes

This snowflake outline makes a bold statement and a nice contrast to filled-in white snowflakes when used together in a design.

1 Start with a circle. To add the arms, draw two parallel lines instead of one at the appropriate points around the circle to form an asterisk shape.

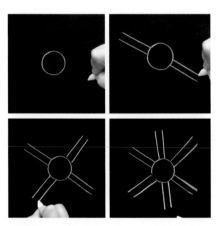

2 Draw two sets of open block shapes on the ends of each double line and enclose the line at the top.

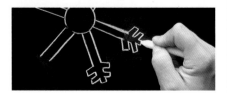

3 Draw two more lines shooting out from the center circle between each main line. Enclose these secondary lines in a similar fashion, but this time, only create one set of blocks on the ends. Make sure they are shorter than the original six lines.

4 Use a cotton swab to erase the circle in the center so all that's left is the snowflake outline. Go back over each stroke with a dull-pointed chalk and heavy pressure to accentuate the outline.

Striped Snowflakes

The interest of this snowflake lies in its unique striped texture.

1 Start with the basic snowflake shape with connecting triangles in the center. Fill in the resulting star shape.

2 Draw diamond shapes between the main lines that connect to the center star and add two small offshoots at the tops of the main lines.

 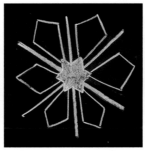 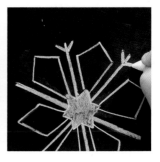

3 With a light pressure, draw thin stripes in the diamond shapes. Redraw the outlines with a heavy pressure to contrast the lightly drawn stripes.

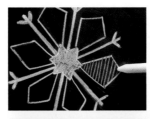

PRO TIP

When drawing snowflakes in a design, fill the empty space around them with small, drawn dots. They will enhance the larger snowflakes and create a detailed, snowy scene.

Part III
Putting It All Together

Test Your Skills

The basics of lettering and layout, shadows and dimension, banners and borders, flourishes, and more: This chapter puts everything you've learned so far into practice. Follow the step-by-step instructions for the two following projects, while altering certain details to make them your own. The lettering styles are meant merely as suggestions, so switch them up and try different looks. To refresh your memory on anything you may have forgotten, just go back and visit the necessary chapter.

Today Is Our Greatest Adventure

An irregularly shaped, but symmetrical border will determine the placing of the other pieces of this design including a banner, two lettering styles, dimension, shading, and flourishing.

1 Mark the center of the board and draw a rough oval to determine where the border should go. Using the oval as a guide, draw each piece of the border starting with the top and working side to side. The shapes of the border should resemble brackets. Pay close attention to how the strokes are lining up on the opposite side and leave a little room between each bracket. Connect each bracket with small triangles. Once you are happy with the border shape, erase the oval guide.

2 With a sharp piece of chalk, add a thin inner border.

3 Draw a curved banner to cross over the border.

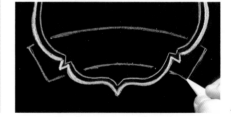

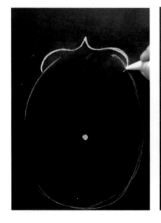

4 Using a ruler or straightedge, line up the wings and base of the banner. The curve should be evenly spread across the border shape. You may have to erase and try again a few times in order to get the placement lined up. Because of this, it's best to avoid overlapping onto your border shape until you have the banner lined up exactly how you want it.

5 Once you are confident in the placement of the banner, fully connect the lines and erase the portion of the border left inside with a cotton swab.

6 Before the lettering is drawn, insert rough guides to make sure you have a good idea where each word will be located. Mark out a line for the word "TODAY" and add a flourish to enclose the words "is" and "our." Add another line for the word "GREATEST." The final word "Adventure" will be placed inside the banner.

8 Complete "TODAY" by making multiple passes on the lettering and adding the serifs. Finish and polish the letters before moving down to the next line, in order to avoid accidentally bumping the design.

7 Since each word in the drawing should be centered, start with the middle letter "D" in "TODAY"—and work your way out.

9 Continue drawing the words in this top-to-bottom manner.

10 Carefully erase the guidelines with a cotton swab and draw extra details, like wispy lines around the flourish. Touch up the lines with chalk to correct any smudges.

11 Shade the wings. Add shadow lines to the word "Adventure" for emphasis.

12 Draw a few flourishes on the corners of the banner and the space between the banner wings. Continue flourishing with looped lines around the design and take advantage of the points where the flourishes meet in a "V" shape to add smaller curls. Add a final layer of flourishes between those smaller curls.

13 Draw small teardrop embellishments to complete the flourish endings on the top, bottom, and sides.

PRO TIP

It may be helpful to take a few steps back from the design to make sure the swirls are evenly balanced around the frame and banner.

Putting It All Together Project #2
Be YOU tiful

This project combines a heart-shaped laurel with a wrap-around wave banner. The shading of the lettering plus the purposeful dust in the heart gives this bold statement a look to match. A simple flourished pattern provides a perfect backdrop.

1 In the center of the board, create a rough heart shape with crisscrossing lines at the end. This will be the branches of the heart-shaped laurel frame.

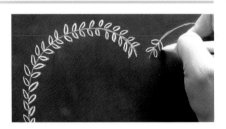

2 Draw the leaves. For this project, keep the leaves relatively the same size with equal spacing between them.

3 Add a wave-style banner that will cross the bottom half of the heart, leaving the tip exposed.

4 Complete the shape. The banner should look as if it is wrapping around the laurel heart.

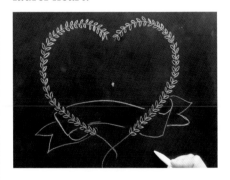

PRO TIP

Do not erase the laurel from the banner until you are confident in the placement.

5 Erase the laurel contained within the banner, but leave the bits that cross through the "folded" areas of the banner untouched.

6 Roughly sketch one top and one bottom line in at the top of the heart for placement of the words "BE YOU." Draw "BE YOU" with the "Y" in "YOU" as the approximate center point. Before moving to the banner, polish and complete the letterforms.

7 Add shading inside the letters for dimension.

8 For even more emphasis, use a wet cotton swab to shadow the words.

9 To make the darkness really stand out, use the corner of a dusty felt eraser to add purposeful dust to the inside of the laurel heart surrounding the words.

10 Add curved lines to fill the empty space between the banner and the letters.

11 Add the letters "TIFUL" into the banner in a coordinating, but different lettering style. Add shading.

12 Shade the banner, paying particular attention to the inside, folded portion that encompasses the laurel. Smooth out the chalk strokes with your fingers.

13 Since we will be adding a flourished background, thicken various sides of the laurels leaves to make them more dramatic. Then, starting at the top of the heart, begin adding "S" shapes with a sharp piece of chalk, alternating their direction and size.

14 Continue making the pattern in this way until the entire space surrounding the laurel heart is covered. Leave a bit of empty space the whole way around the laurel. The "S" shapes should come close to it without touching.

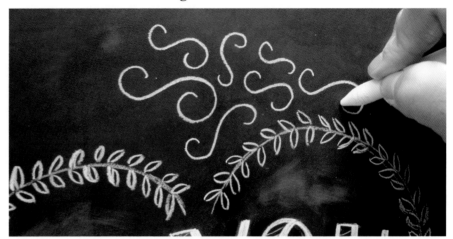

The "S" shapes produce a pretty pattern and backdrop to your heart. Beautiful! Be sure to take a photo before erasing.

Chapter 10

Share Your Skills

This chapter is dedicated to celebrating your new chalk skills with the rest of the world. Turn your drawings into one-of-a-kind greeting cards ,home decor, or printed goods by snapping a simple photograph. Regardless of how you choose to share them, your chalk designs will surely amaze. If you plan to print your cards, keep in mind that a standard greeting card size is 5 by 7 inches. The original artwork does not have to be drawn to those measurements, but you will want to keep the dimension relative so when the image is reduced to size it will still fit nicely. Many online print services are also available. Upload a high-resolution photo and they will print it for you!

Greeting Card Project #1
Just a Message to Say

Part of the beauty of chalk art is its nostalgic, homey feel. This birthday card design mixes vintage and contemporary vibes by featuring a smartphone illustration. Trust me, your friends will think receiving this birthday message is way better than a plain, boring text!

1 A smartphone illustration begins with the shape of a rectangle with rounded corners. Draw another rectangle border inside the first and add a third rectangle for the screen. In the spaces above and below the screen, add the speaker line and the home button.

2 To give the appearance of shininess, draw a few faint diagonal lines across the phone. Give the phone dimension by making the right and bottom sides thicker.

3 Use the space on the screen to write the words, "JUST A MESSAGE to say …" Make the phone look like it's sitting on a table and casting a shadow by dragging a damp cotton swab along the right and bottom sides.

4 Lightly sketch the words "Happy Birthday" to the right of the phone. I chose a script lettering style to give the techy design a sense of whimsy.

5 Eventually, the "B" in "Birthday" should overlap the side of the phone, but for now draw everything except the intersection point.

6 Thicken all of the downstrokes in "Happy Birthday." Use a cotton swab to lighten the descender of the "y" in "Happy" on both sides of where the "d" from "Birthday" intersects.

7 Draw in the intersection and erase the phone to accommodate the overlap. Make sure you are satisfied with the placement before you draw over any finished portion.

Greeting Card Project #2
Sixteen Candles

This birthday card design includes space for the name and age of the recipient. Friends and family will love seeing their names written in chalk. Candles and streamers are used as embellishments throughout to give a celebratory vibe.

1 Using a ruler or straight-edge, begin with two sets of straight lines angled in opposite directions, one on top of the other. Draw a circle by tracing a circular object at the bottom left side of the design. This circle can contain an age, or be customized to include the date instead.

2 Add the word "HAPPY." It should hover over the topmost diagonal line without actually touching it. Cap the word with a candle at the same angle. Sketch in these elements to ensure a good fit before refining.

3 Throughout the design process, add candles and streamers (flourishes) to fill any holes, emphasize the text, and create balance.

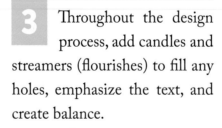

4 Move to the space inside the two diagonal lines, which will contain the word "BIRTHDAY." To center the word, start with the center letters and work out. Instead of an "I," use a drawn candle for fun.

5 Now that "HAPPY" and "BIRTHDAY" are drawn into the design, polish the words by adding dimension to the word "HAPPY" and thickening "BIRTHDAY."

6 Finish the streamers by thickening the bottom portions of the curves and adding dimension where the curves intersect. Add diagonal stripes to the candles and lightly shade the flames. Draw tiny burst lines around the flames to represent candlelight.

7 Complete the top portion of the design by adding dimension to the word "BIRTHDAY" with a damp cotton swab. Be aware of the direction of the drawn shadow of the word "HAPPY" and use the same direction for "BIRTHDAY." Moving to the middle of the design, continue drawing candles and streamers at different angles and directions.

PRO TIP

It is helpful to sketch the entire piece in advance, but it's also fun to allow details to happen naturally. Since the diagonal lines dictated the key words, we can take liberties with the decorations, placing them as we go.

8 Add candles to intersect the diagonal lines drawn in the first step. This layering will contribute to the overall interest of the piece.

9 Draw the recipient's name in the space between the second set of diagonal lines without touching them. Keep this font style thin and simple to contrast the boldness of the "HAPPY BIRTHDAY" lettering.

10 Chalk in little pieces and groupings of confetti throughout the design to add balance where needed. If necessary, add more flourishes.

12 Soften the brightness of the chalk by patting it with your fingers. Add any final confetti specks and you're done. This design makes me want to throw confetti!

11 Using an open block style draw the recipient's age or the date inside the circle and fill in the rest of the circle with chalk.

This is also the perfect space for a little message.

Greeting Card Project #3
You're My Favorite

Illustrated chalk flowers enhance the message of this pretty design meant for someone who holds a special place in your heart.

1 Draw a two-tiered wave banner at the top center of the board. This will contain the words "YOU'RE" and "MY."

2 Roughly sketch the rest of the piece by adding the word "FAVORITE" on a curved line below the banner. Remember to draw in the middle of the word first for accurate centering.

3 Add circles to represent where to place future flower illustrations. Draw lines for the laurels that will accompany them.

4 Starting at the top, add lines and texture to the banners and draw a small rose illustration. It should overlap the banner slightly. Continue working your way down, adding lettering to the banner.

5 Use different types of flower illustrations, like a daisy, in the spaces you designated for flowers in Step 3. Overlapping these floral drawings above and below the banner creates a whimsical effect. Supplement the flowers with drawn leaves and laurel branches.

6 Once the top portion is complete, move to the word "FAVORITE" and refine. This word carries the main emphasis of the design.

7 In a serif lettering style, vary the heights of the letters slightly for an organic feel. Draw an extended "V" that passes the cap line and an extended "R" that passes the baseline.

8 Finish the word "FAVORITE" by carefully erasing the curved guide with a cotton swab and using a sharp point to draw tight shadow lines.

9 Illustrate a lily and daisy under the word "FAVORITE" and draw extended laurels to fill the space and act as an enclosure for your design.

Who wouldn't be thrilled to receive one of these card designs? The same structure can be used for cards that contain a similar number of words. Have fun inserting your own phrases!

Holiday Project #1
A Warm, Fuzzy Design

Our first holiday project depicts the warmth of the season with cable-knit mittens! A cable-knit texture is time consuming and meticulous to draw, but the result is incredibly rewarding.

1 Begin by sketching the mittens in the center of the board. The thumbs should both be facing inside. Stagger the mittens slightly so that they are not directly side by side.

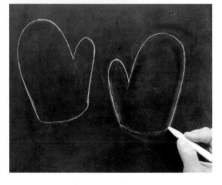

PRO TIP
It may be easier to draw the upside-down "U" shape of the mitten first and then add the thumb.

2 Roughly position the words "Warm Holiday Wishes" around the mittens. Mark an "X" anyplace you want to draw a snowflake.

3 Working your way from the top down, use a bulky script style to fill in the words "Warm Holiday." Using the earlier markings, draw simple snowflake illustrations.

PRO TIP
Simple snowflakes will provide a nice accent to the complex mittens.

4 Begin the cable-knit pattern by drawing two vertical lines down the center of each mitten.

5 On the left mittens draw the outline of the thick, center stitching with tube shapes that look as if they are twisted together.

6 Continue drawing these tubes down the length of the mitten. Keep spacing in mind so the line they collectively create is fairly straight.

  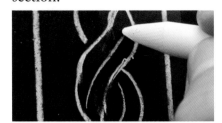

7 Go back through each tube, adding a soft, thin line down the middle of each section.

8 With a light pressure, draw tiny triangle shapes on both sides of the centerlines, working your way up the mitten. The triangles are meant to look scratchy and textured so there's no need for precision. Go back over the cable-knit outline with a sharp point to create a crisp edge.

10 Draw two additional vertical lines on both sides of the mitten, as if there are three lines of stitching on either side, not including the thumb. Fill the space between each line with a series of "X" stitches. This simple motion will make a striking contrast to the center portion of the mitten.

9 Lightly sketch diagonal lines in the spaces between the large cable-knit stitches and the vertical lines you drew. This will create a tightly weaved pattern. Softly pat the space around this new pattern and the cable knit to give the appearance that the cable knit is higher and casting a small shadow.

11 In the same manner, draw lines on the thumb and add a series of "X" stitches along each strip. Polish the shape of the mitten by redrawing the outline.

12 Repeat Steps 5 to 11 on the right mitten, drawing it to be as similar to the left as possible.

13 Draw a mixture of scribbled chalk swirls and softened chalk textures to add fuzzy cuffs to each mitten. Use a cotton swab to create a tiny shadow between the cuffs and the stitching of the mittens.

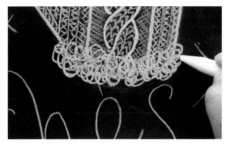

14 Thicken the word "Wishes" and illustrate the remaining snowflakes. Add more snowflakes as needed to fill any holes in the design.

15 Draw shadow lines to the word "Wishes" to add dimension and draw in the mitten strings. They should pass through the "i" and loop into a heart before passing through the "e."

Winter Wonderland Snow Globe A

Snow globes make me think of fairy-tale winter wonderlands that spring to life with just a slight turn of the hand. There's something magical about them. A chalk-art snow globe allows you to create a wonderland that's all your own.

1 Use a circular object to trace a perfectly round circle onto the board. The bottom of the globe should be slightly flattened since it is sitting on a base.

2 Draw the base to contain three layers. Leave enough room in the center layer—you'll be doing something special in this space later.

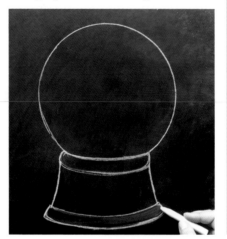

3 Draw the words "let IT snow" on the curve above the globe and thicken the downstrokes.

4 The most important component to a snow globe is snow. Add snowy ground cover to the winter scene and insert evergreen trees. On the side, draw a snowman sitting in the snow.

5 Add the snowman's hat as well as a combination of illustrated large snowflakes and dots of snow. Complete your cute snowman by filling him in with chalk and giving him a scarf. Blot out the coal eyes, mouth, and buttons with a cotton swab and draw his carrot nose.

I wanted the snow globe to have a toylike quality so the illustrations are simplistic and playful. Feel free to refine them to your own liking.

6 Fill in the snowy ground by creating small dips and hills through shadowing.

7 Give the wintry trees snowy caps and a light dusting of chalk texture in sweeping motions.

8 Since this little chalk world is behind glass, lightly add a few curved drawn lines to both sides of the globe. These highlights give the impression of the glass enclosure.

9 Moving to the base, create a spiraled rope on the top layer by drawing a series of upside-down cane shapes. Use your finger to smudge chalk into each separation.

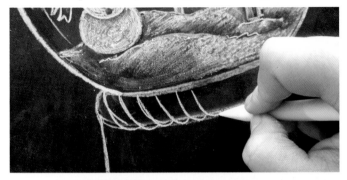 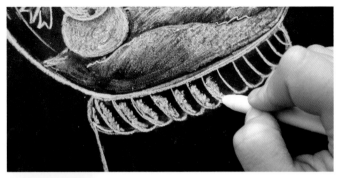

It's a chalk-dusted holiday!

11 Draw and soften the horizontal lines to give the globe some grounding. Use a damp cloth to remove dust in a thick area on the right side of the globe to produce a dramatic shadow.

10 Add soft shadowing to the center and bottom layers of the base as well.

Winter Wonderland Snow Globe B

The snow globe design can transition into other options depending on what suits your fancy or particular seasonal event. As I briefly mentioned before, the center layer of the globe's base offers a great place for customization.

1 Trace a small circle in the center layer of your base and erase any shadowing contained within.

2 Draw your initial in the circle. For another twist, remove the initial and add your name or a message into the base of the globe.

3 Erase the "let IT snow" wording and add a double wave banner that crosses over and wraps around the top of the globe.

4 Erase the design inside the banner. A portion of the loops on either side will be hidden behind the globe. This makes the banner look as though it is wrapped around the globe as opposed to sitting flat on top of it.

5 Draw the words "LET IT SNOW" into the double wave banner in a traditional serif style.

A final holiday chalk tip: Laurels can easily be made to look like holiday greenery! Take the skills you learned in Chapter 8 and supplement flowers with holly leaves and berries for a festive accent to your lettering.

Chapter 11

Celebrate Your Skills!

Hooray! You've made it to the final chapter! We've come a long way and you should be proud. This chapter is dedicated to celebrating your new chalk skills. Whether it's for birthday parties, graduations, or weddings, chalk is a wonderful addition to celebrations of all shapes and sizes. Who knows—you may even want to throw a party just to show off your new chalk techniques. As always, each project is fully customizable and ready to be infused with your unique style. Use the projects as inspiration and get ready to shine!

Party Project #1
Party Invitation

A hand-drawn chalkboard invitation sets the tone for what's sure to be a memorable event. It can, of course, be used for elegant gatherings, but it works particularly well when conveying a rustic-chic vibe, which is the case with this vintage, backyard barbecue-inspired birthday invite.

Use the step-by-step instructions below as a template to customize your own invitation.

1 Begin with an anchor point by placing two horizontal lines across the middle of the board. This detail will be used to delineate between the invitation headline and the party information below.

2 Sketch the outline of a mason jar illustration on the left side of the board, directly over the lines you just drew. Add thin lines at the opening of the jar and top it with a skinny oval for the lip.

3 Draw the shape of a straw coming out of the jar at an angle. Since the jar is made of clear glass, the straw would be seen through it, but only slightly. Leave the portion of the straw inside the glass soft and muted.

4 Draw two flourishes to form an open banner at the top of the design. This will eventually enclose the headline "YOU'RE INVITED." The straw should overlap the bottom flourish for interest.

5 Roughly add three horizontal lines (one curved, two straight) for the lettering placement in the top half of the design. These should go between the headline banner and the two horizontal lines you drew across the middle of the board.

6 Add the outline of a lemon illustration on the right side of the jar.

7 Draw three thin vertical lines as placeholders on the bottom half of the design. This is where you'll include the where, when, and details of the party. Add two more lines at the very bottom of the border.

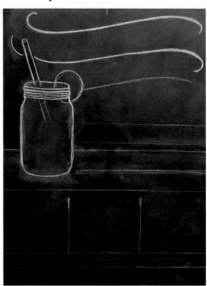

8 With the tentative guidelines and rough placeholders set, go back and letter the headline.

9 Using a sharp piece of chalk, draw line details on each side of the flourish. This will better fill the space as well as add emphasis to the words in the headline.

10 Finish the headline by drawing the letters into a bold, serif style.

11 Draw the second line in the invitation, which includes the words "TO A PARTY FOR." This line of text will follow the same curve as the headline.

12 Add the guest of honor's name in the second line. Use a script style to better fill the awkward, uneven space left under the secondary text. For emphasis, add a flourish at the bottom of the name. This will also create a straighter edge for the word "BIRTHDAY," which will sit on the third line, parallel to our center divide.

13 Give the straw a makeover by adding vintage stripes. Draw in and shade the lemon's sections.

14 Use a combination of drawn lines and chalk smudges to give the appearance of shiny glass and transform the mason jar into a more dimensional illustration. Since the jar is clear, be sure to draw the bottom by lightly sketching a curved line.

15 Once you are happy with the illustration, draw a heart shape in the center and erase all shading within this area. This is meant to look like a sticker on the mason jar. Use the heart to fill in the birthday year.

16 Add the word "BIRTHDAY" on the straight line directly beside the center of the jar. Use a bold, sans serif style with tight shadow lines for the lettering.

17 Turn the original centerlines (the first thing you drew on the chalkboard) into a pretty ribbon accent by drawing scallops on both sides. Erase the straight-line guide marks, leaving just the scalloped ribbon.

18 Fill in this space with small details to form a pattern. Lightly smudge the ribbon where it touches the jar.

PRO TIP

When working with a large amount of text, it is important to avoid looking too cluttered. Leaving small margin spaces will help. Experiment with interesting ways to line up the text in order to get the best fit. Also, use different lettering styles and sizes to break up the information.

19 Add light chalk dust below the jar to ground it and some flourishes for accent.

20 Draw three small versions of the headline banner within the three columns you sketched out earlier. Use a straightedge to line them up . Divide each column by drawing evenly spaced polka dots over the vertical lines. Clean them up with a cotton swab. Draw an oval in the center column, directly over the two horizontal lines at the bottom of the board.

21 Letter the banners with "WHERE," "WHEN," and "DETAILS." Fill in the information under each column. Leave a small margin between the dividers.

22 Add "RSVP" inside the oval. Decorate it with the same embellishment you used on the "ribbon." Draw the phone number and due date. Finish with flourishes to tie everything together.

Welcome Sign

Your guests will certainly feel welcome when greeted with a hand-drawn chalkboard sign. To create a coordinated feel, repeat elements in all your party designs.

1 Begin with a curved banner bridging one edge of the sign to the other. Fill the banner with the word "WELCOME." Leave plenty of space between these letters and the banner lines. Outline each letter and thicken the right and bottom sides to create dimension.

2 Add shadow to the right sides of each letter with a damp cotton swab.

3 Measure a few inches from the left edge and place a mark. Do the same on the right side. The second line of text, "to Daphne's," should start and end at the marks you just drew to ensure centering. Add flourishes to fill the space.

4 Roughly chalk in the third line of text, "PARTY." Instead of the "A," draw a triangle. You'll later turn it into a festive party hat.

5 After these main elements are placed, draw flourishes to fill the empty spaces on both sides of the sign. Return to the second line to polish and finish the letters. Working your way down, thicken the letters of "PARTY."

6 Add drawn, diagonal shadow lines to the letters. Since the party hat is going to be a strong, bold element in the piece, the rest of the letters in the word "PARTY" need to hold their weight.

7 Turn the triangle into a party hat by drawing a cone shape with a rounded bottom and chalk shading. Don't forget to add ribbons to the top of the hat! Add a flower and dot pattern and ground it with shading at its base.

8 Continue flourishing as desired. Add swirls to match the hat and a flower above the word "WELCOME." Draw a flourish on both sides of the banner. Remember to turn the sign upside down or sideways if it makes it easier to draw certain elements that way.

Party Project #3
Photo Booth Sign

Carry the chalkboard theme into the rest of your party decor. A photo booth is a ton of fun and this chalkboard sign will warmly invite guests to participate.

1 Begin with a closed wave banner shape at the top center of the board. Draw two horizontal lines following the top and bottom curves. Instead of a banner, draw this shape to look like a photo strip. Insert the rectangular markings of the photo strip on the top and bottom.

3 Draw the letters into a sans serif style with a thick shadow line for emphasis.

2 Measure the length of the banner shape and divide it into five equal sections. This is how many "photo spots" you'll need to fit each letter in the word "PHOTO". Add vertical lines at the correct measurements. Add the letters.

4 Next, draw the word "Booth" below the strip. Include a second wave banner shape following its curve. Finish the word by thickening the downstrokes and adding texture with a cotton swab.

5 Prop illustrations like a mustache shape, lips, and a bow tie attached to sticks create an amusing design element. Use light strokes to bring line texture to the mustache and draw a pattern on the bow tie. Repeat the same pattern used in the invitation design for a consistent theme.

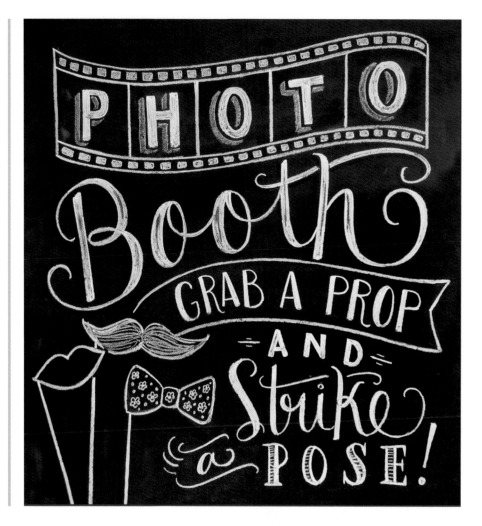

6 Draw the words "GRAB A PROP" inside the second banner and the word "AND" directly below following the curve. Fill the remaining space to the right of the prop illustrations with the words "Strike a POSE." Draw the letter "a" in a small banner. Add flourishes to fill the horizontal space under the bow tie.

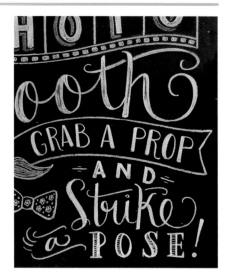

7 Use a damp cotton swab to give the impression that the props are being held up and casting a shadow.

Bake Sale Sign Project
Cupcakes for Sale!

This bake sale sign can be altered for any sort of signage or menu board. Replace the cupcake with any sweet or savory treat to suit your needs. This sign was drawn on a 16-by-20-inch chalkboard, but can be translated to other sizes, including the boards on this book.

1 Using chalk guidelines spaced at a 1-inch margin, and a straightedge, draw a border around the chalkboard.

2 Thicken the border, embellish the ends with swirls and dots, and add another, thinner inner border.

3 Since the word "CUP-CAKES" is the main focal point of the design, make it stand out by drawing it inside a curved banner located approximately halfway down the chalkboard. Eventually, the banner should overlap and cover the border, but for now just line it up correctly and place the elements around it.

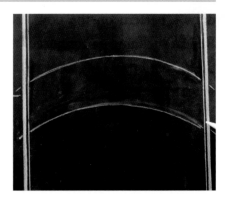

4 Add the cupcake illustration. Begin with the outline of the baking cup. It should slightly overlap the banner. The simplest way to add the icing is to swirl the lines downward, making each loop bigger than the one above it. Use the cotton swab to remove unwanted lines, leaving only the thick icing layers.

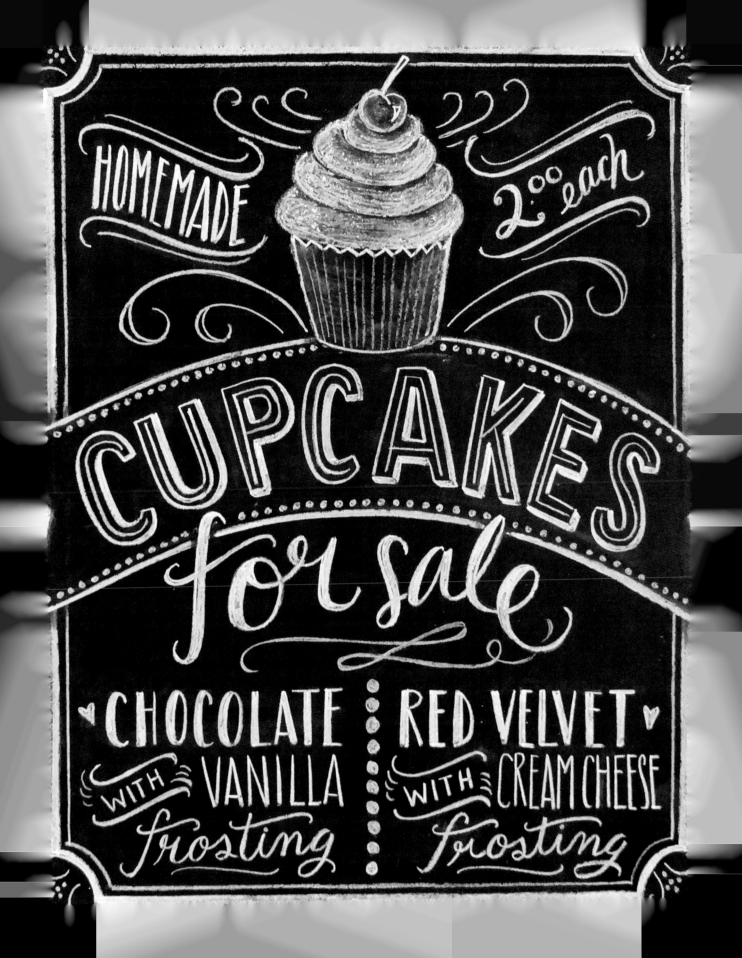

5 Draw flourishes on either side of the cupcake illustration. These will contain lettering. Line them up to be nearly symmetrical.

6 Sketch out the words "for sale" and draw a divider that will separate the details at the bottom.

7 Back to the top of the design, draw the word "HOMEMADE" in the flourish, add line details, and add a cherry stem to the cupcake. It can intersect the border slightly for interest. Fill in the icing of the cupcake by adding chalk dust to the bottom portions of the icing.

PRO TIP

Leave a subtle difference between the icing layers to delineate them. This will require a back-and-forth approach of adding chalk and smudging chalk to get the look just right.

8 Add zigzag lines on top of the baking cup and insert light shading to the sides for a cylindrical appearance. Sketch light vertical lines around the cup for more dimension. Using a damp cotton swab on the right side, give the cupcake a shadow.

9 Add pricing information to the right-side flourish and add thin lines of embellishments around the top and bottom of the cupcake to fill the empty space.

10 Extend the banner past the border and cap it with a cutout triangle shape. Erase the border left inside this space and soften the area of the border where it touches the banner. This will create an understated dimension.

11 Draw a line of tiny polka dots on the inside of the banner near the top.

12 Working from the center out, add the word "CUPCAKES" into the banner with a sharp point. Leave enough room between and around each letter. These thin letterforms are just the first step in the final effect.

13 Outline each letter in the word "CUPCAKES." Thicken the bottom right sides of the letter outlines for dimension. Add another line of tiny polka dots to the bottom inside of the banner.

14 Thicken the downstrokes of "for sale" and carve out the overlapping points (the "f" and the "l") into the banner.

15 Draw a thin flourish underneath for separation.

16 Change the vertical line to a string of polka dots that will serve as a menu divider. Using a straight edge, lightly draw guidelines in order to place the name of the cupcake flavors on a straight line on both sides of the polka dot divide.

17 Sketch the word "CHOCOLATE" using the guidelines. Erase the guidelines with a cotton swab once the word is placed.

18 Repeat the same thing with "RED VELVET" and add the frosting details underneath each type of cupcake flavor.

PURCHASING CHALKBOARDS FOR SIGN PROJECTS

Chalkboards can be purchased in virtually all craft stores. They usually come with a thin, wooden frame. If you feel like being crafty, however, I prefer to make my own chalkboards using chalkboard spray paint. This is an economical option and you can make them in all shapes and sizes to fit your projects. I recommend making your chalkboard out of particleboard or MDF board found in any home improvement store. Real wood can work, but the texture will show through. Particle board will be completely smooth. Most home improvement stores are happy to cut the board to size for you. When you get home, use chalkboard spray paint in a well ventilated area (preferably outside). It is faster and simpler than paint from a can. I've also found it lies much more evenly and creates the desired surface texture for chalk: smooth and clean.

THINK OUTSIDE THE SIGN

Almost anything can be covered in chalkboard paint to create a unique writing surface. Here are a few of my favorite ideas to try:

- Paint a chalkboard platter and use it to serve cookies, cheese, or other items you may want to label. Make sure to use a nontoxic, dishwasher-safe paint.

- If you have an old picture frame lying around, give it new life by painting the glass with chalkboard paint and placing it back in the frame.

- Spray pumpkins with chalkboard paint for a twist on traditional Halloween décor. Try adding a chalk art monogram, maybe even in the spooky lettering style on page 48.

- Paint standard terra cotta pots and make cute planters. Letter the name of the plant or herb on the pot and give it as a gift.

- You can even transform furniture—the fronts of dresser drawers, a small cabinet, or a nightstand—with chalkboard paint.

ACKNOWLEDGMENTS

I would like to thank the following people:

My husband, Mak, for his expertise, opinions, and endless patience with my creating this book.

My parents, Paul and Marcia Henderson, for instilling my creative spirit. Thank you for every sacrifice you made to give me opportunities. I am grateful beyond words for both of you. My family and friends, especially Alec, Neal, Stephanie, Ben, Sandy, Matt, Jillian, Robbie, and Elena. Thank you for your constant love and cheerleading.

Justin, Colleen, Tae, and the entire team at Workman. It is an absolute pleasure working with such incredibly talented, kind people. Thank you for giving me this great opporunity.

To the customers and fans of Lily & Val, whose loyal support has allowed me to continue to draw and do what I love everyday. Without you, this book would not be possible.

And, most important, God from whom all blessings flow.

ABOUT THE AUTHOR

Chalkboard artist and hand-letterer Valerie McKeehan has been drawing and illustrating since childhood. Her passion for commercial art began simply and without pretense: producing hand-lettered signs for her father's business.

Her love of building brand personalities and helping businesses tell their stories creatively through strong visuals led to a career in advertising, working with lifestyle and food brands.

Drawn to the simplicity of chalk and the nostalgia that it inspires, she opened her online chalkboard boutique, Lily & Val, in 2012. Whimsical and undeniably handcrafted, her designs are honest and authentic, at home with their imperfections and unique character.

Working out of her home studio in Pittsburgh, Pennsylvania, at a desk constructed by her husband, she lovingly creates each piece by hand, from sketch to slate, illustrating inspirational quotations or simply depicting everyday subjects, like coffee and cooking, that inspire her work.

Valerie's work has been featured in many publications and noteworthy blogs including: *The Knot*, *Good Housekeeping*, HGTV.com, *Huffington Post*, Real Simple.com, *Flea Market Style*, *Smart*, MarthaStewartWeddings.com, CountryLiving.com, BuzzFeed, Life&StyleWeekly.com, and *Style Me Pretty*.